RICHMOND'S GREAT MONASTERY

The Charterhouse of
Jesus of Bethlehem of Shene

JOHN CLOAKE

RICHMOND LOCAL HISTORY SOCIETY

PAPER No. 6

© John Cloake 1990

ISBN 0 9508198 6 7

Printed by E. H. Baker & Co. Ltd.
86 Lower Mortlake Road, Richmond, Surrey TW9 2JH
Ref. 87415

Front cover illustration: Model of the Charterhouse (see page 13).

CONTENTS

	Page
Introduction	5
The history of the Charterhouse	7
The building of the Charterhouse	10
Shene in lay hands	15
Rediscovering the monastery plan	25
Archaeological evidence from the site	50
Appendix 1. Buckworth-Jeffreys agreement, 1702	56
Appendix 2. Lisle-Bellasys assignment, 1661	58
Appendix 3. Parliamentary Survey, 1649	60
Appendix 4. The other monastic houses of Richmond	65
Notes and references	68
Index	74

LIST OF ILLUSTRATIONS

		Page
	The Charterhouse seal	1
	The second monastery seal	3
Fig. 1	Carthusian monk's habit	6
2	The royal grants to the monastery	8
3	Dr John Colet, Dean of St Paul's	11
4	Cardinal Reginald Pole	11
5	Model of the Charterhouse	13
6	Edward Seymour, Duke of Somerset	14
7	Henry Grey, Duke of Suffolk	14
8	The Duke of Somerset's estate at Shene, 1552	16
9	The 'Little Park', early 18th century	17
10	Thomas Sackville, Earl of Dorset (Lord Buckhurst)	18
11	Helena, Marchioness of Northampton, and Sir Thomas Gorges	18
12	Sir William Temple	20
13	The houses at West Sheen, c1710	22
14	Plan A: 1771	26
15	Plan B: c1750	27
16	Plan C: 1702	29
17	Plan D: 1662	30
18	Restored Carthusian cell at Mount Grace Priory	33
19	Shene Charterhouse, 1635, from Moses Glover's map	34
20	Shene Charterhouse from Richmond Palace, 1562	40
21	The gateway of Sheen, c1770	42
22	The tower of Mount Grace Priory	44
23	Plan E: 1635-49	45
24	Plan F: 1558	46
25	Plan G: 15th century	48
26	Aerial photograph, 1929	49
27	Plan of finds, 1893	51
28	The Charterhouse site and the golf course	51
29	Stones of Shene	53
30	The site today: general view	54
31	The site today: looking north-east from Crown Gate	54
32	The site today: the site of the church	55
33	The site today: the King's Observatory	55
34	Chapel of Richmond Friary, 1562	67

INTRODUCTION

The Charterhouse of Shene was the latest founded, the largest and the richest of all the Carthusian monasteries in England before the reformation. A royal foundation, built close to a royal palace, it was closely associated with and protected by the Crown. It was one of the few monasteries in England (and the only Carthusian one) to be refounded when the English church was reconciled to Rome under Mary I, only to be dissolved a second time when Elizabeth I came to the throne.

This paper gives a resumé of the history of the Charterhouse, of the building works, and of the site and its occupants after the dissolution. It then shows how the original plan of the Charterhouse may be reconstructed from documentary evidence and related to the present-day map.

On my plans was based the model of the Charterhouse exhibited in the Museum of Richmond, and illustrated here. Though I am convinced that the ground plan is approximately correct, evidence for the appearance of the monastic buildings is scarce, and I must confess that my designs for the model owe much to the imagination, guided however by the few clues that do exist in drawings and documents, and by the parallels provided both by contemporary religious buildings and by other Carthusian monasteries.

Much of the material in this paper was previously published as an article entitled 'The Charterhouse of Sheen' in Volume LXXI of the *Surrey Archaeological Collections* in 1977. Since then, however, I have discovered further information on the history of the Charterhouse site and its grounds, and I have reconsidered some details of the plans then published.

In this new version of the paper I have not only corrected what I now consider to have been errors, but I have also added some entirely new material, including a chapter on the archaeological evidence—scarce as it is—which has been gathered from the site and an appendix giving a brief account of Richmond's other two monastic foundations. A lot of new illustrations have also been included.

I hope that in its present form the paper will prove of interest not only to archaeologists and historians of mediaeval monasteries but also to the general reader interested in the history of Richmond—or Shene as it was called before 1501. (I have adopted the spelling 'Shene' as the most usual form used in the fifteenth to early seventeenth centuries.)

John Cloake
Richmond
January 1990

Fig. 1 This Carthusian monk's habit was presented to the Museum of Richmond by the Prior and Chapter of St. Hugh's Charterhouse, Parkminster, Partridge Green, Sussex, in memory of the Carthusian martyrs. Made by a lay brother at the Charterhouse it is, although of modern material, to the exact pattern that was worn in the fifteenth century at Shene and in the other English Charterhouses.

THE HISTORY OF THE CHARTERHOUSE

Shene Charterhouse was one of three monasteries founded in 1414-15 by Henry V around the palace of Shene: an abortive Celestine foundation and the great Brigittine house of Sion, both across the river from the palace, on the boundaries of Twickenham and Isleworth; the Charterhouse itself a little to the north-west of the palace on the Surrey bank of the Thames. Henry V appears to have been fulfilling the charge laid upon his father in 1408 by Pope Gregory XII, but never carried out: that in expiation for the murders of Richard II and of Archbishop Scrope he should found three religious houses.[1]

At a time when English monasticism was being severely criticised for abuses, Henry chose for his new foundations three strict and contemplative orders: the Brigittines, recently founded in Sweden as an offshoot of the Augustinian order, with separate but united communities of monks and nuns and a very strict rule especially in respect of enclosure; the Celestines, a reformed and eremitical order of Benedictines; and the still more eremitical Carthusian order, in which the monks lived most of the time the life of recluses with only minimal concessions to the community life.

The Carthusian order was founded by St Bruno in 1084 at a remote spot in the mountains north of Grenoble called Chatrousse. St Bruno and his six companions lived separate solitary lives as hermits, each in his own log cabin; but they built a small stone chapel in which they could worship together. This set the pattern which the order then followed: solitary living combined with communal worship. The mother house became the 'Grande Chartreuse', and all the houses of the order bore the name of 'Chartreuse' or variants in other tongues. 'Charterhouse' is simply the anglicized form. The latin form 'Cartusia' gave the order its name.

Henry V had an earnest piety, and a great interest in the recluses who combined the life of monk and hermit. It may have been William Alnwick, a former Benedictine monk of St Albans, who was one of the recluses at Westminster, and shortly to be nominated by the King as confessor of Sion, whom the King visited just after his father's death and who prompted him to carry out the obligation.[2] Another recluse of St Albans, Thomas Fishbourn, succeeded Alnwick as confessor of Sion in 1421.[3]

Another powerful influence on Henry V was that of his Chamberlain, Sir Henry FitzHugh, Baron of Ravensworth. While visiting Sweden a few years earlier to arrange the marriage of Henry IV's daughter Philippa to King Eric XIII, FitzHugh had been profoundly impressed by the new Brigittine convent at Vadstena and resolved to found a Brigittine house in England. His manor of Hinton in Cambridgeshire, which he had pledged for his proposed monastery, was ultimately conveyed to the King to be part of the endowment of Sion.[4]

It was probably due to the work on the rebuilding of Shene Palace, largely demolished by order of Richard II after the death there of Anne of Bohemia, that this neighbourhood was chosen as the site of the new foundations. Building of the three monasteries and work on the palace proceeded together under the supervision of the Clerk of the King's Works; and there was demesne land to spare in the royal manors of Shene and Isleworth.

The first charter of foundation for the Charterhouse was granted on 25

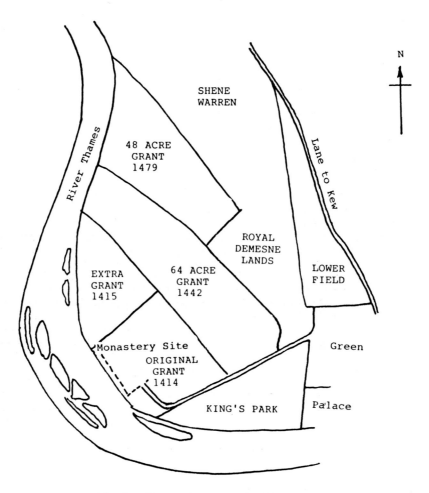

Fig. 2   The royal grants to the Charterhouse.

September 1414; it granted for a Carthusian house, to be called the House of Jesus of Bethlehem of Shene, land belonging to the King on the north side of his manor at Shene, containing 1725 ft in length by 1305 ft 8 ins in breadth, extending from 'Hakelot by Diversbushe on the south to Arniettes lot on the north'.[5] Six months later a revised charter dated 1 April 1415 granted extra lands: the main demesne was now to measure 3125 feet by 1305 feet and extended from Hakelot as before on the south to 'the cross called Crossashe on the north'.[6] In these two charters a great endowment in lands was also established, mostly at the expense of the alien priories recently dissolved.

In 1415 Henry V included in his will a bequest of 1000 marks for the Charterhouse.[7] In 1416 he endowed 'a perpetual reclusory of a recluse chaplain, perpetual and incorporate' within the precinct of the monastery, to be called the reclusory of Jesus of Bethlehem of Shene.[8] At a later date 'a garden newly walled' was rented to the recluse by the Prior and convent of Shene for the sum of 8d a year.[9]

Additional, adjacent, lands at Shene were granted to the Charterhouse by Henry VI in 1442[10] and by Queen Elizabeth, consort of Edward IV, in 1479[11] (see Fig. 2). Their southern limit was marked by the old lane from Richmond Green to the monastery, on the west and north they reached to the river, and to the east they extended nearly to the Green on the south and to the present Isleworth Ferry Gate of Kew Gardens on the north.

Henry VI, Edward IV, Henry VII and Henry VIII confirmed the grants made by their predecessors and granted further lands and privileges,[12] and the Charterhouse flourished under royal patronage and protection until the Act of Supremacy in 1534. The Prior and monks of the London Charterhouse took a strong stand in opposition to the oath of supremacy, but the Prior of Shene was a more complaisant character, who induced the monks to give way to the royal demand.[13] In 1538 the Shene Charterhouse appears to have made a 'voluntary surrender' of its site and all its property; but no deed of surrender has survived, so the precise date of Shene's first dissolution remains unknown.[14]

The site of the monastery was granted to the Earl of Hertford, later Duke of Somerset, and was subsequently in the occupation of the Duke of Suffolk. Both in turn forfeited their rights by attainder and when the question arose in Mary's reign of finding a home for a refoundation of Carthusians, Shene was in the hands of the Crown, though lent to the Dowager Duchess of Somerset.

After the dissolution some of the Carthusian monks in England made their peace with the new regime and became parish priests, some no doubt returned to a secular life, a few went into exile abroad to continue their profession. Among those who found shelter in the Charterhouse of Bruges was Father Maurice Chauncy of the London Charterhouse. When Queen Mary reconciled her country to Rome, the Prior of the Grande Chartreuse suggested that some of the English Carthusians at Bruges should attempt the restoration of the order in England. Chauncy, with another monk and a lay brother, set out in June 1555 and found the climate very favourable to his enterprise. Reginald Pole, Cardinal Archbishop of Canterbury, had close connections with the Shene Charterhouse, while the Controller of the Queen's Household, Sir Robert Rochester, was the brother of one of the Carthusian martyrs of the London Charterhouse. He and Pole introduced the monks to the Queen and commended their project. While waiting, Chauncy was joined by some other monks and lay brothers who had remained in England. Eventually the Queen recovered Shene from the Duchess of Somerset[15] and on 17 November 1556, Pole and Rochester handed the site over to Chauncy and his flock. Rochester set to work to help them with the task of reconverting it to monastic use.[16] On 31 December 1556 Pole appointed Chauncy Prior, and on 26 January 1556/7 the Queen formally re-granted the buildings and lands to the monks.[17] The Grande Chartreuse confirmed Chauncy's priorate a few months later.[18]

The restoration was short lived. In November 1557 Rochester died and was buried in the church of the Charterhouse. A year later, on 17 November 1558, the second anniversary of the delivery to the monks of the Charterhouse, Queen Mary and Cardinal Pole both died. Some of the brethren of Bruges had warned Chauncy against undue optimism: 'quicker than you look for, you will all be hurled suddenly from your buildings'.[19] The inevitable legislation quickly followed Elizabeth's accession, and was as quickly followed by commissioners enforcing the second dissolution. At the commissioners' third visit on 1 July 1559 the monks were expelled.[20] Through the intercession of the Spanish Ambassador they were granted safe-conducts to return to Flanders.[21] The subsequent history of the community of 'Sheen Anglorum' does not concern us here. It retained its identity and its existence until 1783, thirteen years longer than the 'site of the late dissolved monastery of Shene'.

THE BUILDING OF THE CHARTERHOUSE

There are few details available of the building of the Charterhouse, but it was a recognized part of the King's 'great work' at Shene, for the Clerk of the King's Works, John Strange, and the Comptroller of the King's Works, John Hertishorne, were put in charge, as they were of the work on the Palace itself, begun in 1414.[22] Walter Walton (d 1418) was Master Mason for the monastery, and Stephen Lote for the palace.[23] It was probably in early 1415 that Henry Beaufort, the Bishop of Winchester, within whose diocese Shene lay, commissioned Benedict Nichols, Bishop of Bangor, to lay the foundation stone.[24] By the time that King Henry V left on his first trip to France in autumn 1415 the monastery appears to have been consecrated and its completion was to be speeded: 'which house we have ordered to be maintained by our bishops . . . the which house, not yet fully finished, should be brought to completion with the greatest possible speed.'[25] In his will made in the same year the King bequeathed 1000 marks for the completion of its 'greater house' intended for forty monks.[26]

Although it would seem that building was well under way already in 1415, the first references to the procurement of labour and materials specifically for the Charterhouse occur in March 1417.[27] The implication of these references is of a seasonal reactivation of building activity, with flooring or roofing taking an early place in the year's programme of work. There may be an additional indication that the monastery was virtually completed in 1417 in that the General Chapter of the Carthusian Order formally incorporated 'the new plantation of Jesus of Bethlehem at Shene' in that year, and promoted the rector, John Wydryngton, to be Prior.[28] Such a formal step was normally delayed until the physical arrangements for the monastery were satisfactory. By June 1419, £867 4s 11¾d had been spent on the monastery at Shene and £1290 6s 5½d on the two sister foundations on the Middlesex bank of the River.[29] Some work was however still in hand at Shene three years later.[30]

The materials used must have been much the same as at the palace, brick for some buildings, stone or part brick and part stone for others, and almost certainly some lath and plaster timber-framed out-buildings, possibly on freestone foundations. Some Caen stone was used, and substantial quantities of ragstone, chalk, tiles, etc., were brought from the demolished royal manor house at Sutton (in Chiswick), from which source came also 436 lbs of lead for the roofing of the reclusory.[31]

Some further building or alteration was put in hand in 1457 when the General Chapter instructed the Prior of Mount Grace Charterhouse to send his lay brother, William the carpenter, to Shene and to let him remain there until the convent could go into new cells.[32] Later again the church was enlarged by the addition of a chapel with three altars.[33]

Apart from the deductions which can be made from later evidence, which are considered below, the only direct information extant on the size or shape of the buildings is a somewhat confused description by William of Worcester who visited Shene in the reign of Edward IV. He states that there were about thirty houses for monks within the four-sided cloister; that its length was 200 paces, so that it contained 800 paces in all; that the height of the cloister walls was '3 yards, i.e. 9 feet'; and that the nave of the church, apart from the choir, was

Fig. 3 (Above) Dr John Colet, Dean of St Paul's, by Holbein. (British Museum)

Fig. 4 (Below) Cardinal Reginald Pole. (British Museum)

60 paces long.³⁴ John Harvey, in the introduction to his edition of William's *Itineraries*, calculates that the latter's 'pace' or 'step' is equivalent to about 21 ins and is probably 'the combined dimension of his two feet placed heel to toe'.³⁵ This gives a cloister enclosure some 350 ft square, and a nave some 105 ft long. The former is a little larger than that at the London Charterhouse (about 340 ft by 300 ft) and larger than the irregular quadrilateral of the Mount Grace cloister (of which three sides were just over 230 ft and the fourth side 273 ft).³⁶ The dimension for the church is surprising. The Carthusians did not normally go in for large churches or long naves, for their rule was centred on the contemplative rather than the celebratory aspects of monastic life, on the cell rather than on the church. At Mount Grace the nave was only 43 ft and the whole church, including a presbytery east of the choir, about 120 ft; at the London Charterhouse the whole church was some 97 ft long, and it had no true nave at all but rather a vestibule at the west end. That there was a nave at Shene seems to be confirmed by the account of the reconstruction work carried out on the refoundation of the monastery in 1555/6, for the choir had been completely destroyed, while the walls of the 'rest of the church' were still standing.³⁷

Two other building works are recorded before the dissolution. On 30 June 1466, King Edward IV granted to the Prior and monks a licence to make a subterranean conduit from the spring called 'Welwey alias Pickwelleswell' to their house, and to repair the pipes when necessary. The grant explains that Henry V had granted them a conduit from the spring called Hillesdenwell, but that the yield of water had proved insufficient.³⁸ As the Priory seems to have survived on the Hillesdenwell supply for fifty years, the insufficiency suggests that an improved plumbing system resulting in a greater demand may have been associated with the work on 'new cells' in 1457. The only detail we have of the water supply is at a much later date: in the 1649 survey we are told that the various houses on the site 'are very well accommodated with water which is brought and conveyed unto them through several small pipes of lead branched from one great pipe of lead from the stop-cock or conduit head on Richmond Green unto a great cistern of stone placed within the said wall of Shene.'³⁹

About 1518-19 John Colet, the famous Dean of St Paul's, built himself a house within the gardens of the Charterhouse, but hardly had he finished the house when he fell ill of 'the sweating sickness' and died there.⁴⁰ In this house were later to live briefly two still more notable figures.

Reginald Pole, who had been a scholar at the school run by the Charterhouse from the age of seven until he was twelve, went back to Shene when he returned to England from Italy in 1527 and occupied Colet's house there until he went to Paris in 1529.⁴¹

The house then provided a home for a month for the disgraced Cardinal Wolsey, who moved in early March 1530 from the keeper's lodge in Richmond Park where he had briefly stayed on the King's sufferance 'to the rooms in the Charterhouse which Colet had built', and remained there until he set out for his last journey north on 5 April. Cavendish says that he 'went every day to the Charterhouse there, and in the afternoons he would sit in contemplation with one of the most ancient fathers of that house in their cells'.⁴²

Three months after Wolsey's departure, Reginald Pole, still a layman, but later to become a Cardinal, returned from his mission to Paris. He once more set up his abode in Colet's house at Shene. When he departed in 1532 he left some of his goods behind. They were still there when the monastery was dissolved.⁴³

The physical restoration of the monastery in Queen Mary's time was the work of Sir Robert Rochester. Chauncy's narrative says that the building had not been destroyed and, although 'much altered into a fine mansion' could be reconverted to monastic use without too much difficulty. The work which Rochester put in hand included rebuilding the choir of the church 'from its foundations' and restoring the rest of the church which was 'miserably shattered and decayed, the walls only standing and those very ruinous', and completely rebuilding the chapter house which had been demolished. In three years 'a good number of cells and a cloister' were also completed.[44] The restored monastery was however a much smaller foundation than the body of 40 monks which Henry V intended, or the body of 30 for whom houses had been built around the original cloister, and Chauncy can have seen neither point in nor possibility of restoring this original cloister for his small fellowship consisting, in 1556, of only nine choir monks and three lay brothers. That only a small cloister was rebuilt on the north side of the church and chapterhouse is one of the conclusions of the study that follows.

Fig. 5   A model of the Charterhouse of Shene about the year 1450. The model was sponsored for the Museum of Richmond by Solaglas Ltd, whose offices in the King's Observatory are adjacent to the Charterhouse site. It was designed by John Cloake and built by Scale-Link Ltd.

Fig. 6 Edward Seymour,
Duke of Somerset.

(British Museum)

Fig. 7 Henry Grey,
Duke of Suffolk.

(British Museum)

SHENE IN LAY HANDS

After the first dissolution in 1539, the whole site was leased in farm to Edward Earl of Hertford, brother of the late Queen, Jane Seymour, and uncle of the heir apparent, Prince Edward.[45] A grant to Hertford was conveyed by letters patent of King Henry VIII on 7 April 1541;[46] and six months later on 26 October the sale to the Earl for £168 of the lead on the buildings of Shene Monastery 'estimated by the King's plumber at 42 fodders' is indicative of a considerable progress of demolition.[47] We know however that the walls of the nave of the church still stood and certain other buildings, enough—though converted into a stately home—to provide a nucleus for the 1556 restoration. Two inventories of the lands held in farm by Hertford make it possible to plot the lay-out of the estate.[48] (See Fig. 8)

In 1547, on King Henry's death, Hertford induced the council of 'executors' set up by the King's will to nominate him Lord Protector and Duke of Somerset. One of his first acts was an exchange of lands: he surrendered Shene to the King in exchange for various lands, including Osterly and Isleworth 'late of Syon'.[49] But he appears to have continued to lease Shene on a year to year basis, and still held the annual farm in January 1551/52 at the time of his attainder and execution.[50]

Shene was then granted to Henry Grey, Duke of Suffolk.[51] Stow visited Shene during the reign of Edward VI, 'Henry Grey then Duke of Suffolke there keeping house', and was shown the alleged body of King James IV of Scotland among a lot of building rubble.[52] In July 1553, after the failure of the attempt to put Lady Jane Grey on the throne, her sister Katherine 'was sent to Shene, a palace the Suffolks had acquired from Northumberland after Somerset's fall, and remained there alone for her parents and Jane and Guildford Dudley were still in the Tower'; on 31 July Suffolk and the Duchess left the Tower for Shene.[53] When Suffolk and his unfortunate daughter and her husband were finally executed in 1554, Mary lent Shene to Protector Somerset's widow, the lady who was so obstinate about giving it up when the Queen and Pole wished to replace the Carthusians there.[54]

Similarly, after the re-expulsion of the monks in July 1559, Elizabeth restored Shene to the widowed Duchess of Suffolk. The Duchess however died within the year on 20 November 1559. After her funeral on 5 December her daughters Lady Katherine and Lady Mary Grey took communion and then returned to the Suffolk palace at Shene 'in their chariot'.[55]

The next occupant was Sir Richard Sackville, who soon found himself responsible for the custody at Shene of the Queen's cousin, Margaret Countess of Lennox, and her son the Earl of Darnley while the Earl of Lennox languished in the Tower of London.[56] Sir Richard's son Thomas, Lord Buckhurst, the future Earl of Dorset, in 1568 was saddled with another unexpected guest, the Cardinal de Chatillon, brother of the French Huguenot leader, Admiral Coligny. Buckhurst left Shene in some disgrace, having in the Queen's eyes failed to provide properly for the Cardinal's reception.[57] For some years thereafter Shene seems to have remained in the direct occupation of the crown, and was used as an annexe to Richmond Palace. Finally, in 1584 it was granted to Sir Thomas Gorges and his wife Helena Marchioness of Northampton, on condition 'that at

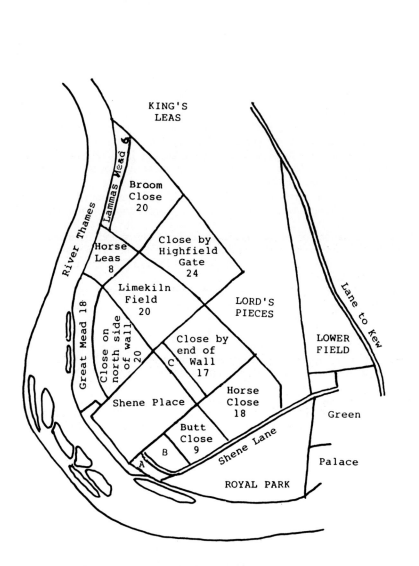

Fig. 8 The Duke of Somerset's estate, 1551. (numbers indicate acreages)

A Rockless Mead 1½
B Close by Crown Gate 4
C ?Robin Hood's Walk 1½

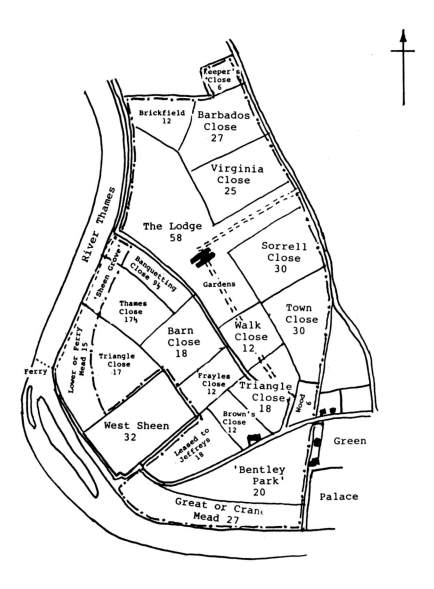

Fig. 9 The Little Park, early 18th century.

Note 1. The identification of some closes is conjectural (numbers indicate acreages).

Note 2. The seven-acre 'Sheen Grove' was surrendered for enclosure in the Park in 1637; the Great Meadow was included in the West Sheen grant in 1638.

Boundary of the Park as enclosed by James 1   — · — · — · — · —

Fig. 10 Thomas Sackville, Earl of Dorset, formerly known as Lord Buckhurst. (British Museum)

Fig. 11 Helena, Marchioness of Northampton, and Sir Thomas Gorges. (detail from a genealogical tree) (British Library)

her Majesty's access to Richmond her officers may have lodging there, saving to the farmer [i.e. Gorges] the house called the Pryor's House.[58]

During Gorges' tenure most of the former monastery lands were taken back by King James I in 1604-05 to add to his new Royal Park.[59] (See Fig. 9.) Gorges died on 30 March 1610, but his wife lived on until April 1635. The Marchioness in 1612 granted a lease of Shene House to Henry Prince of Wales, who probably wanted it as temporary quarters in view of his project to rebuild his seat at Richmond Palace. After the Prince's death, King James decided to retain the house and continued to pay an annuity to the Marchioness in compensation.[60] On 10 November 1625, however, a lease was granted for 27 years to Sir Robert Douglas, later created Viscount Belhaven.[61] He held it until 1638[62] when a new grant was given, for life, to James Duke of Richmond and Lennox.[63]

Stables for the Palace use had been erected—or converted from the the monastic buildings at the western end of the Charterhouse site—in Queen Elizabeth's reign. These were added to during the early seventeenth century. Henry Prince of Wales had a riding school built, and extra stabling and coach houses were erected. Some of the other old monastic buildings were converted into separate dwellings. From about this time the spelling 'Sheen' becomes more usual, and the name of 'West Sheen' begins to be applied particularly to the hamlet which was developing within the former Charterhouse walls.

Lennox managed to hold on to the monastery site during the Civil War; as with most royal supporters he had to pay a heavy fine to keep his estates,[64] but the £40 levied on account of the site of West Sheen monastery availed him nothing when Parliament decided to raise more money by selling off all the Crown estates. In January 1649/50 a detailed survey was made of the monastery,[65] and although it was not, unfortunately, accompanied by any plan, a comparison of its detailed description of the buildings with the drawing by Moses Glover made in 1635[66] provides the most important link in the process of reconstructing the plan of the monastery. The house was sold on 29 May 1650 to Alexander Eaton for the sum of £2233 11s 9d[67], and it would appear that he rapidly sold or leased it to Lord Lisle who was in occupation by March 1651.

Such sales were set aside on the restoration and in July 1660 the grant to Edward Villiers of the keepership of the largely destroyed royal palace and of the old park and various manorial offices included the keepership of the late Monastery of Sheen.[68] Lennox had died in 1655 and the site was again available for disposal, but Lord Lisle's interest therein was recognized and legitimized. On 7 August 1660 a lease for 60 years was granted to Philip Sidney, Viscount Lisle (later Earl of Leicester).[69] An important development now took place.

Eaton possibly, but more probably Lisle, seems to have pulled down many of the old buildings including most of the monks' houses which still existed in 1650. In any case a new mansion existed by December 1661, and Lisle proceeded to divide up the property, assigning the new house and about a third of the land to John Lord Bellasys.[70] In January 1662 he also assigned to Bellasys the meadow land outside the monastery site[71] and in March Bellasys acquired a new lease of these properties in his own right.[72] Further deals followed: part of the meadowland was reassigned to Lisle and then in September and October 1662 respectively Bellasys assigned his holding and Lisle part of his to William Lord Crofts,[73] so that the property was now divided between Crofts and Lisle. The deeds relating to these involved transactions, particularly the assignment from Lisle to Bellasys, in which the boundary between the two parts is largely drawn with reference to 'ancient walls', are very helpful for the monastic plan.

In the spring of 1665 William Temple acquired from his friend Lord Lisle a lease of one of the houses on the latter's property,[74] within the confines of the Crown Court (one of the walls of which 'fayled' in 1666 and was 'newly raysed'

Fig. 12 Sir William Temple—a print engraved by P. Vandrebanc after the portrait by Sir Peter Lely. (British Museum)

by agreement between Lisle and Bellasys). Temple wrote to Lisle in August 1667 from abroad: 'The best on't is that my heart is so set on my little corner of Sheene that while I keep that, no other disappointment will be very sensible to me; ... my wife tells me she is so bold as to enter into talk of enlarging our dominions there....'[75] Whether he got an enlarged leasehold property at that time or not, in 1670 when he was again in England he purchased a house (presumably the one he had been leasing) from Lisle and spent £1000 on improvements to it and to the garden, and in the next year laid out a further £500, which was a gift from his father 'rather for ornament than for use ... to make the front of the house uniform'. In 1675 he purchased another house in Crown Court from Lisle. The total cost of the two houses and improvements was £6000.[76]

About 1675 Henry Brounker acquired Lord Crofts' property,[77] and petitioned for a new lease.[78] An arrangement was made whereby a reversionary lease for the whole site was granted to trustees nominated by Brounker and Temple,[79] and they on 3 August 1676 duly divided the property up again by assignments to Brounker, Temple and Lisle.[80]

In 1678, on 27 August, John Evelyn 'dined at Mr Hen. Brounchers at Abbey of Sheene, formerly a Monastery of Carthusians, there yet remaining one of their solitary cells with a cross; within this ample enclosure are several pretty villas, and fine gardens of the most excellent fruits, especially Sir William Temples lately Ambassador into Holland and the Lord Liles son to the Earl of Leicester, who has divers rare pictures above all that of Sir Brian Tukes of Holbein.'[81]

In 1683 Temple, by then in retirement from active public life, acquired a third house at Sheen 'with two small tenements on each side the gate of the said Crown Court'. At the same time, and by agreement with him, one Robert Rossington took, and subsequently sublet, the remainder of that part of Sheen still in the ownership of Lord Lisle (then Earl of Leicester). But the neighbours fell out. Henry Lord Brounker, who was constantly vying with Temple, and exchanging barbed witticisms with him, over the respective merits of their art collections, had hitherto been a peaceable if rather obstreperous neighbour and Temple, with some reluctance, having a great regard for his privacy, had allowed him to make a gate into Crown Court. They quarrelled over a remark at a dinner party, and Brounker turned really nasty. In a combination with Rossington he claimed a right of way for carts and carriages through Crown Court, he broke down more of the wall and set up large gates, and when Temple objected he threatened to build an outhouse as close as possible to Temple's mansion and 'burn turfe therein and stink him out of his house and garden'. Temple was resorting to legal action and drafted a petition to the court, which is the source of most of the above information.[82] The case does not appear to have been settled; perhaps it was not proceeded with, for on top of this unpleasantness came a real domestic blow when Temple's only surviving daughter died at Sheen in 1684. The 'little corner' had lost its sweetness, and following his son's marriage in 1685, Temple divided his estates and retired to Moor Park at Farnham in 1686 leaving Sheen to young John and his bride. He returned to Sheen in 1688, perhaps as a consequence of Brounker's death in January of that year, but again disaster struck. In April 1689 John Temple, a week after being appointed Secretary of War, committed suicide by drowning himself in the Thames at Westminster. It was shortly after this blow that Sir William Temple first engaged Jonathan Swift as his secretary. Swift was not long at Sheen (though long enough to make himself very ill with a surfeit of apples that summer) for by the end of the year the Temples left Sheen for good.[83]

Brounker bequeathed his house at Sheen to Sir Charles Lyttleton; and

Fig. 13   The houses at West Sheen, c1710.
The group of houses in the centre of this detail from Jan Greffier's painting of Syon House probably represent the mansions at West Sheen. Greffier portrayed individual buildings accurately, but composed them in a picture with little regard to topography. In the left foreground here is a part of the grounds of Richmond Lodge. Higher up, on the left, is the tower of Richmond Church and immediately adjacent to it is New Park at Petersham! Petersham Church can be seen on the right.

Reproduced by permission of the Duke of Northumberland.

shortly after Sir Charles took up residence we have another glimpse of Sheen and its personalities from John Evelyn (29 March 1688): '... with Sir Charles Littleton to Sheene an house and estate given him by my Lord Brounchar, one who was ever noted for an hard, covetous, vicious man, had several bastards; but for his worldly craft and skill in gaming etc few exceeded him: coming to die, he bequeathed all his land, house, furniture etc entirely to Sir Charles, to whom he had no manner of relation but an ancient friendship, contracted at the famous siege of Colchester 40 years before. It is a pretty place, fine gardens and well planted. ... After dinner (at his house) we went to see Sir William Temple's, near to it: the most remarkable thing is his orangerie and gardens; where the wall fruit trees are most exquisitely nailed and applied, far better than in my life I had ever noted. There are many good pictures, especially of V Dykes, in both these houses, and some statues and small busts in the latter'.[84]

After 1692 came another major change of occupation. On 26 March of that year Sir John Buckworth purchased the former Brounker estate for £4000 from Sir Charles Lyttleton.[85] Within the next decade Mr John Jeffreys bought up all the rest of the monastery site from Sir William Temple, from the executors of the Earl of Leicester (the former Lord Lisle, who died in 1698), and from the assigns of Robert Rossington.[86] On 30 December 1702 Buckworth and Jeffreys agreed to an exchange of some lands for their mutual convenience and finally settled the quarrel over rights of way started nearly twenty years before between Temple and Brounker.[87]

From then on the property remained divided between the Buckworth and Jeffreys families, but the Jeffreys' holding included several houses and was subdivided accordingly. One of the Crown Court houses which Temple had occupied was apparently pulled down to make way for new stables. The old 'great house' was leased to a Mr Long and then to Lord Blundell, but by 1749, when a new lease was sought, it was 'empty and ruinous' and Jeffreys sought and was granted permission to pull it down. To the north-east of this was a house occupied by Walter Cary in 1749 and then by Elizabeth Cary, his widow, until 1764 when it was leased to one John Reeson. Cary added some additional buildings and Reeson carried out extensive repairs. On the eastern part of the site, a third house was occupied successively by Charles Selwyn, John Jeffreys himself (in 1749-50), the Earl of Ashburnham and James Hunter. It was described in 1765 as an old building, 'poorly built and lacking repair' except for the south-east corner which had been blown down in a gale and rebuilt but was 'not yet finished within'.[88] Title to the Buckworth house passed in due course to Lieutenant Francis Buckworth of the Royal Navy and from him to Charles Buckworth who obtained a new lease in 1760. It was however leased at that time to one Andrews, calico printer.[89] For a few years the calico printing works at West Sheen were a major feature of Richmond's economy.

By 1764 however it was obvious that the new King, George III, had his eye on the property, and the lease to Reeson contained provision for compensation if His Majesty wished to resume the property at the end of a five year term. The King was already thinking of replacing the adjacent Richmond Lodge by a new palace, for which he commissioned a series of plans from William Chambers. Although a newspaper reported in 1767 that the plan of the new palace was marked out and that it was to be executed rapidly,[90] work was not started until 1770, and never got beyond construction of the ground floor walls; but the Observatory, which still stands, was erected just to the north of the monastery wall in 1769, Chambers again being the architect. There is a collection of working papers and notes from the Crown Estate Office dated about 1765 in which the titles and sub-titles to the lands on the monastery site are examined, and calculations made concerning the compensation to be paid to Jeffreys when the sub-lease to Reeson could be broken in 1769.[91] Jeffreys' two remaining houses are described in some detail; the old and rather decrepit one on the north-east (which we may call for convenience the 'Selwyn house') had four rooms and two closets on the ground floor with four rooms and a gallery over them, and kitchen and offices with servants' quarters over. There was a stable for seven horses and sheds for two carriages, and the ground comprised $2\frac{1}{2}$ acres of pasture and 6 acres of garden. The 'Cary house' was larger, with four good rooms, servants' hall, kitchen, pantries and 'other commodious offices' on the ground floor, and 'nine convenient lodging rooms' above. A separate building contained washhouse, laundry, servants' rooms and a 'long gallery now called the Billiard Room'. There was a coach-house for two carriages, stabling for 12 horses, and $8\frac{1}{4}$ acres of land.

In 1769 the Crown resumed possession and in the next two years the houses and buildings were demolished. Only a greenhouse and a shed or two were still standing when a survey was made of the royal estate in 1771, but they can only have had a few more months of existence before the last vestiges of the monastery were, together with Richmond Lodge, razed to provide more pasturage for His Majesty's cattle. Work on the new palace was abandoned when the King moved to Kew in 1772 and it too was demolished some years later.

REDISCOVERING THE MONASTERY PLAN

The deeds of lease and assignment and the Parliamentary Survey are our principal written sources of evidence. They are supplemented by some eighteenth century plans and three drawings, only one of which is of any real use in considering the layout. The earliest piece of graphic evidence is a distant view in the background of a drawing of Richmond Palace from the river made by Antony van den Wyngaerde in 1562 (see Fig. 20).[92] The rough sketch is very detailed and apparently accurate and is indeed rather more informative than the finished drawing, but the cluster of buildings which it shows are, save for the great tower, hard to disentagle or identify. The second, and far most valuable drawing, is the one by Moses Glover illustrating his map of the Hundred of Isleworth made in 1635, which is preserved at Syon House. It lacks complete authority, for some of the details in this map (as those of Richmond Palace) which can be checked are inaccurate, but the general layout of the palace is fairly accurately depicted and the bird's eye view of the monastery can reasonably be accepted as a reliable, if rough, representation (see Fig. 19). The third drawing shows only the main gate (see Fig. 21).

A painting of *circa* 1710 by Jan Greffier, also at Syon House, gives a good impression of some of the mansions by then built on the site; and some eighteenth century prints also provide distant glimpses of the 'pretty villas', but only sketched in rough outline.

The plans are, unfortunately, relatively late in date, when there was little left of the original buildings on the site. There are two which are well detailed and appear accurate, of 1749 and 1759 respectively, associated with new leases to John Jeffreys and Charles Buckworth.[93] The first shows only Jeffreys' part of the grounds; the second the whole site and the adjoining meadows. The detail in it corresponds closely with that shown, on a smaller scale and with less precision, in John Rocque's maps of Richmond Gardens and the environs of London.[94] A little later we have the detailed survey of the Royal Manor of Richmond and of the Royal Gardens of Richmond and Kew in 1771.[95] A few outbuildings and boundary walls are all that were by then left on the monastery site, but the newly built adjacent Observatory is shown and this, with the general (but subsequently somewhat altered) line of the river bank, suffices to relate the location accurately to the modern Ordnance Survey map.

Our starting point is the 1:2500 Ordnance Survey plan, onto which we can plot the boundary walls and buildings shown on the 1771 survey plan. In addition to the perimeter wall, this gives us the main east-west line dividing the property and a number of north-south walls in the gardens, Plan A (see Fig. 14).

With these to provide a frame of reference, we can plot in the dimensions[96] and other details shown in the Rocque maps and the plans of 1749 and 1759, locating with fair accuracy four main houses and more outbuildings. We thus arrive at the result given as Plan B (see Fig. 15).

Starting from Plan B as a basis, the four plots of ground exchanged in 1702-3 between Sir John Buckworth and John Jeffreys[97] (see p.23) can now be identified. They are illustrated in the text of the agreement (summarised in Appendix 1) by little outline sketch plans on which dimensions and areas are given. We can plot these on to the plan. The Frayles, the Buckworth kitchen

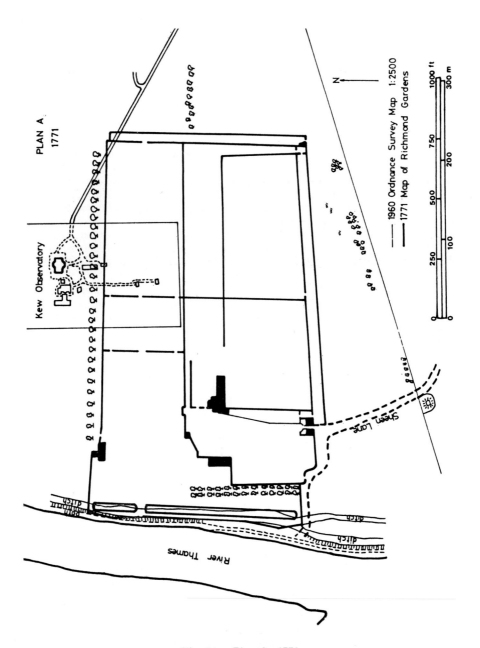

Fig. 14   Plan A: 1771

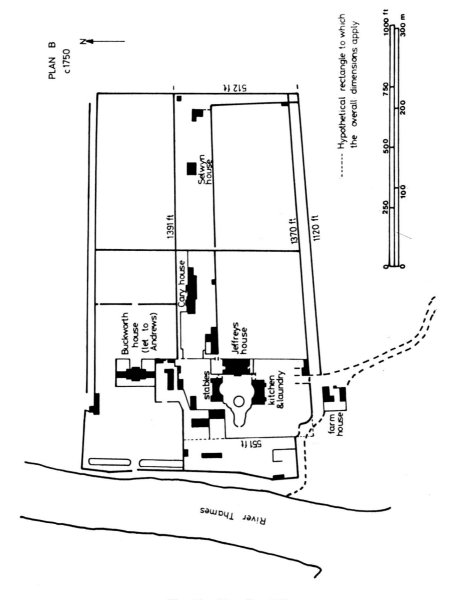

Fig. 15 Plan B: c1750

garden and drying yard fit exactly where they are supposed to; and we can insert Lady Bellasys' drying yard as to fit neatly into the later boundary and give a probable straight line boundary before the exchange. We can now also identify Crown Court, and tentatively locate two other houses—a little brick house at the end of Lady Bellasys' drying yard, which was transferred to Buckworth, and Lady Bellasys' house, which adjoined it. As we know that one of the houses which Temple occupied was pulled down to build new stables, it is appropriate that the probable site of Lady Bellasys' house is where the stable block is shown on the later plans. One other building was handed over to Buckworth: 'an old building at the end of the yard in the occupation of Sir John Buckworth'. The probable site for this is shown on the plan, but the justification for this choice can more easily be considered at the next stage.

We now have, as Plan C (see Fig. 16), the boundaries as they existed for forty years, following the division of property between Lord Crofts and Lord Lisle in October 1662. The assignment from Lisle to Crofts of 12 October 1662[98] included, in addition to what Lisle had previously assigned to Bellasys, also land between the monastery wall and the Thames, land between this last parcel and 'the gates which open into the lane from Sheen to Richmond', and 'the Red Barn and the building behind it of two rooms one above the other'. The two parcels of land listed separately suggest that extra land may have been recently enclosed—some of it along the riverside being perhaps the result of new floodbanks and reclamation.

The next step is to trace the boundary of the ground assigned by Lisle to Lord Bellasys in the first division of the site on 12 December 1661 (see Plan D, Fig. 17). The text of the deed of assignment[99] is very informative and is given in extenso at Appendix 2. The most important part is the course of the 'ancient brick wall'. This is described as 'beginning at the south-east corner of the said Viscount Lisle's stables called the Green Stables next the courtyard called the Crown Court going south, abutting east on the said Crown Court, unto the cross wall about thirty feet from the Great Gate entering unto the said court, thence turning westward toward the River of Thames it abutteth south upon the way and footpath towards the Ferry. . . .' Our previous identification of Crown Court enables us to start this line in the correct place and to follow it in detail until it turns south by the Frayles. The precise point at which it turns west from the wall by the Frayles is uncertain, but here the wall runs to the north of the ground and house in the possession of Master Wormall, and as this must be roughly in the location of the 'Cary house' of 1749 we can reasonably equate Master Wormall's with it. Past the Wormall house, the boundary suddenly jumps northward 64 ft to go around the 'Monks' Hall', which remains in Jeffreys' hands. There is no clear evidence to indicate that the main boundary line between the Lisle and Bellasys properties was subsequently altered in this particular sector, but a 32 ft strip was excepted from the grant to Bellasys to provide a lane to the Frayles (from the garden next the Monks' Hall). A short stretch of this is clearly visible on Plans A and B, and we can therefore continue it up to the Frayles and locate the 'ancient wall' 32 feet south of the later boundary. A curious little kink in the boundary shown in the 1749 and 1771 plans gives us a clue to the location of the 64 feet of boundary which ran due north beside the Monks' Hall. Although this little rectangular salient does not extend into the Bellasys area for the whole remaining 32 feet which we would expect, it is not otherwise explained. This salient is however 'at the end of the yard occupied by Sir John Buckworth' and has a building adjacent to it, in Buckworth's possession, on the 1759 plan. If the latter were (or had replaced) the old building at the end of the yard which changed hands in 1702, we would have about 32 feet for the depth of the salient before 1702. We may thus fix here the approximate site

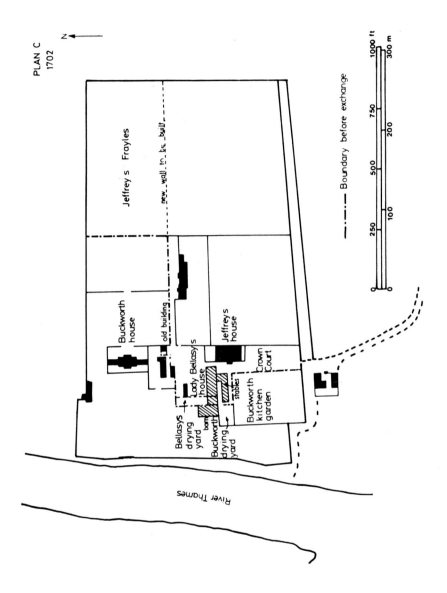

Fig. 16   Plan C: 1702

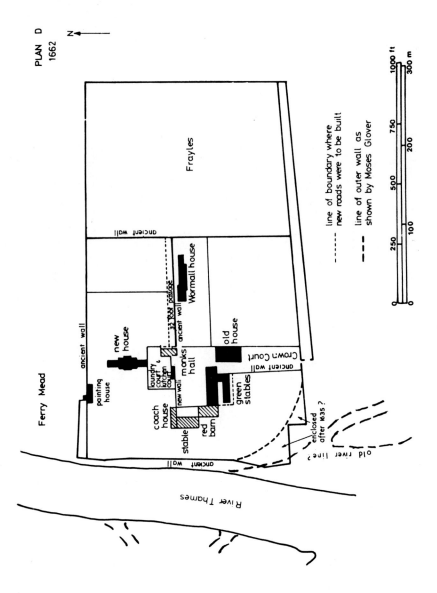

Fig. 17 Plan D: 1662

of the Monks' Hall, and continue now by 'new walls' separating the Laundry Court and Kitchen Court of Lord Lisle's (new) mansion from his 'other houses and courts' until we reach 'the north-east corner of a little piece of ground adjoining on the backside of a timber building once used as coachhouses and since for stables'. Our line then turns south and runs immediately west of the Red Barn (which we noted in the 1662 assignment) to the south-west corner of the Green Stable and turning east along the south wall of the Green Stable returns to the starting point. Another strip, this time of 15 feet in width, was reserved for a roadway behind the Green Stable.

The correct interpretation of this last sector of boundary is difficult to determine. The Red Barn, assigned to Crofts in 1662, appears to have been reserved by Lisle for himself the year before. If the identification of 'Lady Bellasys' Drying Yard' in the 1702 exchange was correct, the Red Barn must lie on its west side, and is probably the barn noted as adjacent to 'Buckworth's Drying Yard'. But its shape and size we do not know. Nor do we know which was the 'back' side of the coachhouse-stable building. The intepretation I have chosen is one of many possibilities—it is influenced by the layout of the buildings in the Moses Glover drawing, discussed below (see Fig. 19).

The line of the wall from the Gate to the riverside and parallel with the river bank is not specified in detail in the 1661 assignment and it would be strange that so detailed a description should ignore the irregularities of line which are so clearly visible in the later plans. Although this might be simply because, in dealing with the established outer circuit wall, precision was less necessary than in defining a new boundary, it seems more likely in the light of the 1662 assignment by Lisle to Lord Crofts that the old wall mentioned in the document ran at least in part to the eastward of the later boundary. The northern corner however fits exactly with the dimension (53 perches and 14 ft) given in the assignment as the length of the north wall up to the wall of the Frayles. If the Moses Glover drawing is to be credited, the south-west section of the wall swept round in a broad arc from the gate to the river bank in 1635. As suggested above, the extra pieces of land by the river, and between the south-west corner and the Crown Court gate, were probably enclosed between 1635 and 1661. Lord Lisle may have done this after his acquisition of the site. He was responsible for enclosing the long narrow slip on the south side of the monastery site, though it had been cultivated as a garden for some time previously. The rolls of the Manor Court of Richmond for 1 March 1651 relate that 'the slips of ground on the south side of the Frayles wall lying between it and Richmond Park, lately enclosed by Lord Lisle with a pale hath been of antient time a garden plot taken out of a private ground by Sir Thomas Gorges the owner of the Priory of Sheene by a grant from the Crown, and since that time used and occupied by him and his tenants together with the said priory. . . .' This long narrow garden is noted also in the 1649 survey.

So far we have been dealing with houses and their out-buildings, courts and gardens, and the only hint of previous monastic occupation is the 'Monks' Hall'. But the 1650s were a period of major destruction of old buildings and construction of new ones from the old materials, and the Parliamentary Survey of 1649, which we must next consider together with the Moses Glover drawing of 1635, brings us much more closely into the context of a partly ruined, partly adapted monastery. Before continuing it would therefore be useful to consider what we might reasonably expect to find.[100]

There was a uniformity of concept, if not of exact plan, about Carthusian foundations which was quite distinct from that of the houses of the other religious orders. The large church, dormitories, and large refectory of the normal monastic plan, even the hospital, had no function or place in a Carthusian house.

Instead, the nucleus was a large enclosed court or garth around three sides of which the monks' cells stood like rows of small detached houses each with its little garden plot, divided from its neighbours and from the world outside the cloister by walls high enough to prevent all casual intercourse. The cell or house was usually of two storeys, standing in the front corner of its little garden (see Fig. 18). Typically, the ground floor would be divided into a lobby with doors into the cloister and into the private garden and with a small stair to the upper floor, a living room with fireplace and a small bedroom and still smaller study; the upper floor would be a workroom. At the far corner of the garden against, or rather projecting through, the outer circuit wall would be a privy. Outside the wall would be a drain with running water. The path from the house to the privy was normally protected by a pentice. A similar pentice might run along the inner side of the garden wall against the cloister. Next to the door leading from the lobby into the cloister would be a hatch, designed with a right-angled bend so that food could be passed in from the outside without any contact between the monk and the monastic servant who would bring it from the kitchens.

These cells would normally stand on the west, north and east sides of the great cloister garth, and a cloister walk or pentice would connect them and be continued right around the fourth, south side. Here might be found one or two more cells at the eastern end, then the church with the chapter house contiguous to it on its north side. The sacrist's cell would be nearby, and probably the monks' washing place, and the cells of the prior and the procurator (who was the general manager of the monastery and who in particular directed the lay brothers and the servants). Also in the southern range, at its western end, or at the southern end of the western range, would be the small frater used only on Sundays and feast days; and beyond it, outside the cloister enclosure, the kitchens and associated buildings such as bakehouse and brewhouse. The south-west corner was therefore the point of access to the cloister and the point where the quarters for the lay brothers and the monastic servants would be found. In earlier Carthusian buildings the lay brothers might have a separate cloister on the same pattern as that of the monks, with their own individual cells and their own chapel; in later foundations their quarters were more usually in common buildings round a small court or courts. Beyond to the west or south, or both, would lie the guest houses and the workshops, stables and barns, either around a great outer court (as at Mount Grace) or a series of small courts (as at the London Charterhouse). We have said that the prior's cell and the procurator's would be near the church, but they were not necessarily within the cloister. They would be conveniently situated near the south-west access for their greater communication with the world outside the cloister. At London the prior appears to have moved from an original cell within the cloister itself to a more commodious 'new cell' south of the chapter house and south-east of the church. The church itself would be of modest size with only a short nave or vestibule, and without aisles or transepts but possibly with a series of chapels. If any expansion of the numbers of the original foundation took place, new cells would have to be built and these might be around a smaller cloister, possibly with access to the great cloister at its south-eastern corner.

The Charterhouse of Mount Grace in Yorkshire, built at the beginning of the 15th century and thus a near contemporary of Sheen, has survived, though in ruins, sufficiently to enable an exact plan to be drawn. One other, at London, preserves some relics of the monastic buildings and, in later buildings, other features of the original plan. Wartime bombing, and subsequent excavation for rebuilding, uncovered further remains of monastic foundations and enabled a

Fig. 18   Sketch of restored Carthusian cell at Mount Grace Priory, Yorkshire, by the author, 1975.

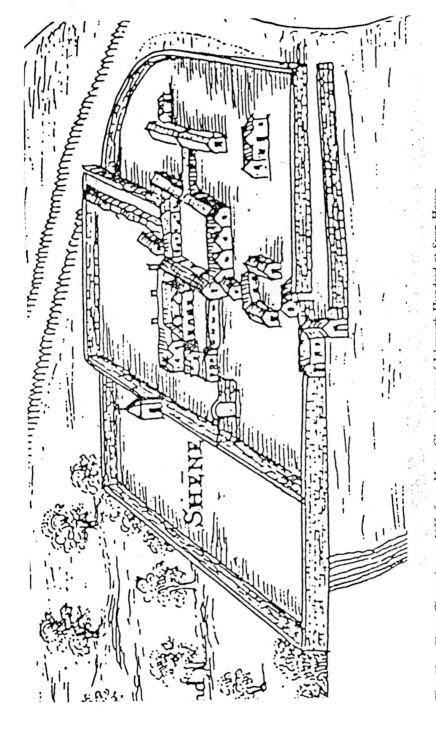

Fig. 19 Shene Charterhouse, 1635, from Moses Glover's map of Isleworth Hundred at Syon House. Reproduced by permission of His Grace the Duke of Northumberland.

fairly accurate plan to be reconstructed by Professor Knowles and W. F. Grimes (see note 100).

From the plans of these two Charterhouses we may take some typical dimensions, remembering that both were smaller foundations than Sheen, Mount Grace being in origin a 'single' unit of prior and twelve monks, London approximately a 'double' unit and Sheen in intention a triple unit (though it may never have achieved its full intended strength of 40). At Mount Grace the great cloister was an irregular quadrilateral with three sides just over 230 ft and a fourth (the east) side of 273 ft. Fifteen cells stood round the cloister, the cells and gardens not all identical in plan but for the most part some 48 ft square. A small extra cloister to the south-east contained five additional cells. At London the great cloister was 340 ft by 300 ft, containing (including three at the east end of the south side) twenty-four cells and gardens of some 45 ft square. Here again some extra cells were added at the south-east corner. The church at Mount Grace was 120 ft by 25 (varying to 27) ft, with a 40 ft nave and 65 ft choir and presbytery, and with a central tower. The church at London was some 97 ft by 38 ft (disregarding the several contiguous chapels) with only a small western vestibule, and its belfry tower stood not above the church itself but above the vestibule of the chapter house, north of the end of the chancel. The chapter house at Mount Grace measured some 30ft by 24 ft and lay alongside the choir of the church, with entrance directly therefrom; that at London (externally 47 ft 6 ins by 26 ft) lay separate, north-east of the church, with entrance through the vestibule below the tower. The frater at Mount Grace, at the western end of the southern range of the cloister, west of the Prior's cell, measured some 30 ft by 17 ft internally; that at London, at the southern end of the western range, north of the original Proir's cell, measured 45 ft by 24 ft.

With these plans as our guide we may now look at the 1649 Survey,[101] of which the text is at Appendix 3, and the 1635 drawing (Fig. 19), which shows the buildings in bird's eye view from the north side. There appear to be two courts, a smaller more crowded one on the left, one slightly larger on the right linked to a long straight range by a cross piece forming a kind of H. Separate outbuildings stand on the near (north) side. There is little likelihood of extensive rebuilding during these mostly troubled years between 1635 and 1649—and no evidence of it, so we may assume that the buildings as shown in the drawing illustrate pretty closely, if not exactly, those described in the survey. The survey tells us that part of the old church (very ruinous), the Prior's Lodging, the Monks' Hall, and at least five 'anchorites' cells' are still in existence. Where can we find these on the drawing? We have already identified the Crown Court, which forms part of the grounds of the Prior's Lodging, as being, in part at least, that long narrow court from the gate into Sheen Lane up to the 'old great house'. No gate is clearly visible on the south, far side, of the drawing, but the long narrow court is plainly there and by its north-east corner stands a separate building. Here then is the Prior's Lodging, the house pulled down by John Jeffreys about 1750. The great garden which lay on the back side of the building and which, with the Crown Court and 'a little court before the door' contained five acres, is without doubt that area of ground on the far (south) side of the monastic buildings as seen in the drawing. Defining this area by the boundaries already shown on our plan give some $4\frac{1}{2}$ acres, which is not near enough to give positive confirmation but not so far off as to rule out this identification as impossible. The Survey describes however a mansion far too grand for a Carthusian monastic dwelling, even for the influential Prior of Shene. But we must remember that this has been a nobleman's home for a century; it was the building reserved for the personal use of Sir Thomas Gorges when he had to lodge the officers of Queen Elizabeth's court.[102] Clearly it would have been enlarged, but why should it have formed the nucleus of the stately home in the first place? It seems reasonable to suggest that here is the house of Dean Colet, which was later used as lodgings by Pole and Wolsey, to which the Prior might have moved when it stood empty, and in which Prior Chauncy would almost certainly have set up his headquarters and dwelling when the monastery was refounded.

The Survey tells us next of a small tenement with a small garden lying between the Prior's Lodging and the south wall of the old church. Although it is used for kitchen and washhouse in 1649, its plan, with two rooms and a gallery below, and two rooms above, sounds like a possible monastic cell and is indeed identical (except for the gallery) with the description of most of the buildings which are identified as former cells. Here is probably the Procurator's cell.

Now we have the south wall of the church more or less fixed and we must expect the site of the church to form part of the southern side of the great cloister. The 'Cary-Reeson' house of the 18th century does not appear to exist in 1649, or it would surely be described at this point of the Survey, and would be related to the site of the church. So we can safely assume that the large building at the far side of the left-hand court seen in the drawing represents what was left of the old church itself. It does not appear ruinous, and indeed seems to have some chimneys which would suggest that a part of it had been converted into use as a dwelling. Perhaps its final ruination was a development of the Civil War period. This position for the church makes sense in relation to the access from Crown Court to its south-west and in relation to the Prior's Lodging, but if we are right so far where is the Great Cloister we should expect? The left-hand court in the drawing is actually the smaller of the two. We must however recall that the buildings we are considering are the remains, not of the original foundation, but of the Marian refoundation, and that Prior Chauncy had to rebuild cells and cloister for his small community. It is likely that, taking the restored church and rebuilt chapter house as the basic south side, Chauncy would have planned a small cloister to contain no more than a dozen cells at most. It is possible that the north-south wall which much later divided the garden of the Buckworth mansion (see Plan A, Fig. 14) followed the line of the enclosing wall on the east side of this small cloister. In the absence of any other indication, I have adopted this hypothesis.

Next in the Survey are listed three buildings, all too large for monastic cells, all of substantial construction (one part stone and part brick, the others wholly of brick) and all used as homes. The second belonged to the Surveyor of the Prince's Stables, the third had a garden at the south-west end of the great barn, and it was considered to be a part of the stable complex reserved for palace use. We shall follow the example of the surveyors and return to the stables and barns later; suffice it now to say that they fit well enough with the ranges of buildings on the right hand (west) side and in the foreground of the drawing (and that the U-shaped building in the foreground is probably the 'Great Barn'). We can therefore assume that the parliamentary surveyors have turned westward from the church into the right hand court shown in the drawing. Here we may have the converted remains of a courtyard housing the lay brothers, and perhaps some guest houses and kitchens. Putting our trust in Moses Glover and also in the methodical approach of the surveyors we may note that the far (south) end of this court appears in the drawing to consist of three distinct buildings; and that the first of the three houses noted by the surveyors was 'formerly two'. If we allot two of the buildings shown to this house, the next one listed in the Survey—that of the Surveyor of the Stables—must be the one on the corner; and the third, 'very commodious', one with the garden which lies to the south-west of the great barn is probably to be found at the other end of the court—

probably the building with the four gables in the drawing. Its little garden is probably the small parcel of land between the four-gabled building and the U-shaped one in the foreground.

The surveyors list next the Monks' Hall, a stone building of one large room, with two cellars below. The 'Monks' Hall', or at least its site, we have already tentatively identified from the 1661 assignment, and it is due north of the Prior's Lodging, on the east side of our hypothetical lay brohers' court. Our surveyors thus appear, having listed all the buildings whose entrances were in the first court, to be turning back towards the monks' cloister and the area of the church. A building known as the 'Monks' Hall' in such a position is surely, by comparison with the London and Mount Grace plans, the frater, and the description of it as a large single room with cellars below is clearly appropriate.

After the frater we come to a little tenement with three rooms below and two above and then to a range of buildings described as being on the north side of the old church. We are clearly moving eastwards along the south side of the cloister court. The small tenement with the extra room is the likeliest candidate for the original Prior's cell. The next building, 'Lady St John's Lodging', departs from the usual pattern in having one room below and four above; its little garden lies to the north wall of the church. Here perhaps, in the 'one room below', we have the chapter house. It must have been a sizeable room for the floor above it to be divided into four. The building is part of stone and part of brick. Several of the buildings were of this mixed construction, and it proves nothing, but it is compatible with the hypothesis of an original stone monastic building with an upper storey added later in brick. The next building listed is called the Gallery; part of it is wainscotted and now divided into three rooms, and it adjoins 'to the last mentioned tenement on the south'. If this means that it lies to the south of Lady St John's Lodging, then the chapter house, if such it was, would seem to have been physically separated from the church, by some sort of passageway or side chapels, later converted into a dwelling. A far likelier interpretation is that Lady St John's Lodging was to the south of the Gallery. Then the Gallery could fall into pattern as part of the cloister walk, now closed in to form a small dwelling, and the little garden north of the church could lie adjacent to the chapter house. Although the Moses Glover drawing is at its most obscure at this point, we could possibly identify as the Gallery that low building with three windows and a door on the far side of the cloister court, and the higher roof between it and the church as that of the upper storey added to the chapter house to give Lady St John her lodging. The little garden probably lay to the right (west) of the chapter house.

The surveyors turn next to the remaining cells. The first one noted, like most of the others, contains two rooms below and two above and has, as we would expect, a little garden. Its 'long shed' is no doubt the pentice by the garden wall. Next follows one which seems to be double size—four rooms below and four above. But it has 'two little gardens', which reveal it as not one cell but two, built semi-detached either to solve the problem of the corner site (compare the north-east and south-east corners of the London Charterhouse plan) or in the centre of a side. Three more cells follow in the Survey, two on just the same pattern, and the last with two rooms below and only one above. As all these cells have been used as dwelling houses, it is more probable that the single large upper work-room of the typical Carthusian cell was sub-divided in all but one case than that there is a real difference in pattern in the Sheen cells. The location of these cells on the plan causes difficulty, for only two appear clearly as distinct units in the drawing (on the left-hand, i.e. east, side of the cloister court). But three of them have extra land attached in addition to their gardens. The double unit has $2\frac{1}{2}$ acres of 'the old churchyard'; the last but one has a rood of ground, also 'part of the old churchyard', lying to the east of the great barn; and the last has an acre and a half of the old churchyard 'between the last mentioned parcel of land and one other parcel of the old churchyard used for a nursery', together with a strip of land 35 ft wide by Crown Gate and another little piece of ground 30 ft wide adjoining the north wall of the church. To take this last piece of land first, it presumably lay near the chapter house, perhaps on the other side from Lady St John's 'little garden'. One of the two no doubt represented the wash-court or laundry, which lay to the west of the chapter house at Mount Grace, and to the east of it at London.

Together with the parcel of land in the old churchyard 'used and planted for a nursery', which is listed separately without an area given, but which from its value would seem to be not more than an acre, we have between 4 and 5 acres and a rood of land which is described as the 'old churchyard'. Although it does not automatically follow that the shares of the old churchyard were contiguous to the cells to which they became attached, it is possible so to divide the area on this hypothesis and keep our surveyors pursuing a methodical course. First however, we must settle what is meant by the 'old churchyard' and here we must look back for a moment to the original monastic buildings before and after the first dissolution. The inventory of the Duke of Somerset's lands taken in January 1551 refers to a parcel of land called the Churchyard containing by estimation 4 acres. The term 'churchyard' carries the implication of burials, and it was Carthusian practice to bury the deceased brethren in the cloister garth. The area which would be enclosed by William of Worcester's 350 ft square is only a little over $2\frac{3}{4}$ acres, but if we take this as the dimensions of the cloister walks and add some 50 ft on each of three sides for the cells, we have an area of just over 4 acres. As the original cells were all demolished, this suggests that the 'old Churchyard' of which we are speaking is the original great cloister. A part of the $2\frac{1}{2}$ acre garden however appears to have lain to the east of the church, outside the cloister. This probably accounts for the somewhat larger total in the Survey.

And now we return to that 'ancient wall' which formed so convenient a boundary in 1661. The quadrilateral bounded by the wall on north, east and south and by a continuation of the east wall of Crown Court and the Prior's Lodging on the west gives us, by measurement on the plan, dimensions of 500 ft on the north, 490 on the south, 400 on the east and west; say 495 ft by 400 ft as an average. Allowing our 50 ft for the demolished cells and their gardens on north, east and west, we get a close enough correlation with William of Worcester's measurements not to stretch credulity (see p.12). We shall return to these calculations later, but we must now have another look at those six cells of Prior Chauncy's cloister still standing in 1649.

Leaving the south-east corner of the court, by the chapter house, we can see on the drawing two isolated buildings of small size on the east side of the court, and another which seems to stand behind them a little to the north side of the church. These buildings might be the two single cells and the double cell. But if the double cell is the corner unit, we have the difficulty that the surveyors seem to have departed from their methodical sequence, so I think it more probable that the separate buildings shown in the drawing are the double cell and a single cell, and that there is one other single cell in the corner by the church. The $2\frac{1}{2}$ acres attached to the double cell could conveniently be the whole area in front and behind the brick wall with the gate shown to the left of the cloister court. The north side of the cloister court appears in the drawing to consist of a single long, low building, which is apparently unmentioned in the survey. It might be the other two cells, but one would have expected Glover to draw them detached where they showed so clearly. However, the similarity of this building to the postulated 'Gallery' at the far side of the court is striking, so it may be no more than a part of the old cloister walk. The line between the brick wall with the gate and the end of the central range of buildings between the two courts which seems oddly broken may be that of the original rear wall of the cells at this side, demolished before 1635. Or perhaps Chauncy never finished building the cells on this side of the cloister. The two other cells listed are perhaps to be found at the end of the range of buildings on the right hand (west) side of the cloister court. It appears on the drawing to be continuous, but it is of course end on. If we can place the cells here, then the one with its rood of ground to the east of the great barn fits into place and its separately listed 'little outhouse used as a stable or cowhouse' might be the small building behind the U-shaped Great Barn. The $1\frac{1}{2}$ acres belonging to the last cell would be most of the rest of the area between the north outer wall of the monastery and the cloister court, together with the cloister court itself; and the 'nursery ground' would be a small strip between this parcel and the $2\frac{1}{2}$ acre ground to the east.

Having completed the cloister court, the surveyors turn to the outbuildings and surrounding land, and note first two items in this category which they have already passed—a small building with an acre of land lying between the Crown Court and the Little Frayles, occupied by the ferryman of Sheen Ferry, and the nursery ground. The former is probably that area which was exchanged in 1702 when it was part of Sir John Buckworth's kitchen garden. The surveyors continue, round the outside of the buildings, to the northern end of the enclosure where there is a small gate called the Water Gate, with a lodge, before turning back to work steadily through the Prince's Stables. The Moses Glover drawing shows other buildings outside this gate and a long court formed by a double wall leading from the gate towards the river. The outside buildings are probably the farm house to which Jeffreys was guaranteed access in the 1702 exchange, the long court, or part of it, representing the bulge at the north-west corner of the site previously noted as a probable 17th century addition, no doubt containing at some time a small dock and quay.

The first of the buildings belonging to the Prince's Stables to be noted by the surveyors is the Great Barn, which we have come across twice before. An open timber building of eleven bays, it is probably the U-shaped building in the foreground of the drawing, a situation which ties in with the previous two references. The barn used for riding 'the King's great horses' is listed next, a five-bayed building which may be the free-standing one towards the north-west corner of the site. The great horses, sixteen of them, were stabled in a brick building which may be the north end of the range on the west side of the first court. (The stables would be approached from outside, not from the court itself, so would not have been listed earlier, when the surveyors were in this court.) Stables for the hunting horses and the coach horses came next, probably going south down this range, with the saddler's office at the south end, close to the house occupied by the Surveyor of the Stables. The far end of the parallel range, and perhaps the cross-piece of the 'H' would then form the Great Stables for eighteen horses, with the Smith's Forge projecting at the south end; and the near end of this western range may be the coach house, which adjoined the north end of the Great Stable. These identifications are far from certain, and other interpretations are clearly possible, but the precise identities of these buildings, probably erected in the late 16th or early 17th century, do not directly affect the monastic plan. It seems possible, however, that the general outline of the western court may embody the earlier layout of a courtyard round which were the lay brothers' quarters, guest houses and kitchens, offices, etc.

The area in which these stable buildings stood was called the Little Frayles, a name which (as Little Prayle) appears as early as 1540 when the area is given as $3\frac{1}{4}$ acres. In the 1551 inventory of Somerset's holdings it does not appear, but

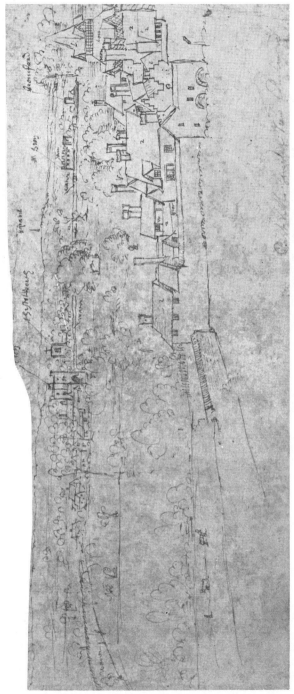

Fig. 20 Shene Monastery from Richmond Palace, 1562. A. van den Wyngaerde (The domestic buildings of the Palace are in the foreground; in the background, from left to right, can be seen the curve of the River, the monastery buildings, with the big tower, the tower of Isleworth Church, Syon and Brentford).

(In the Ashmolean Museum, Oxford, LIV12aR, reproduced with permission.)

its place seems to be taken by a parcel of 2 acres of land 'lying next the Slawterhous' and a parcel of one acre 'lying next the Flesshehall'.

Although these names, which I have not found in any other document, probably relate to the usage of buildings during Somerset's occupancy, the date is sufficiently near to the Dissolution to warrant consideration of the possibility that they may describe monastic buildings. Despite the strictness of the Carthusian rule and its absolute ban on meat, there is nothing wholly impossible about the existence of such buildings in the monastery, for both the monastic servants and the guests might eat flesh. There was a flesh-kitchen at the London Charterhouse and expenditure on flesh figures in the London accounts.[103]

At the east end of the monastery site were the Great Frayles or Prayle of some ten acres (sometimes given as eight acres) in area, a name which also goes back at least to 1540. This was not built on, except for the dovecote mentioned in the 1649 survey. It is possible that this is the building shown in the Moses Glover drawing as standing on the wall between the Great Frayles and the garden of the Prior's Lodging. But the building does not look particularly like a dovecote and it appears to be surmounted by a cross. It does not seem to be particularly noticed in the survey, but could it be the reclusory, perhaps converted into a dovecote, or even into two dovecotes, as the Prior's Lodging also has one listed among its outhouses? Could it indeed be the one cell with a cross which was still standing when John Evelyn visited Sheen in 1678?

At first sight, and if we can trust the scale of Glover's drawing, this building might even be a relatively low church tower with squat spire, but it seems to stand too far to the south-east to have any close connection with the church. Indeed, were it a part of the church buildings one might expect the survey to have contained rather more than the single note that 'there is a part of the old Church of Shene yet standing but very ruinous and fit for nothing but to be demolished and taken down, the materials wererof besides the charge of taking down the same are worth £10'. There was a church steeple with a bell in it still standing at the time of the grant to Gorges in 1583, but the word 'steeple' can mean simply a tower and does not necessarily imply a spire—and we have another candidate for the church tower.

In the Wyngaerde drawing of 1562 (see Fig. 20), just after the second Dissolution, a large tower, with corner turrets, appears. It looks like a large gatehouse of typical 15th or early 16th century pattern and has been interpreted as such by a series of writers who identify it with the 'ancient gateway' which Manning tells us was 'the last remains of the Priory' and was 'taken down about the year 1769.[104] The 1771 plan shows what appears to be a gate with two lodges, and might be an arched gateway, though there is no sign of any of this in the Rocque plan, and only the eastern lodge appears on the 1749 plan. The Lisle-Bellasys assignment in 1661 mentions 'the Great Gate entering into the [Crown] Court' and Temple in 1683 acquired 'two small tenements each side the gate of the said Crown Court'. There is however no mention of any gatehouse building in the 1649 survey and no sign of any gatehouse, let alone a tower, in the Moses Glover drawing. The picture [105] which we have of the gate fits well with the 1771 plan, and with the description of Temple's acquisitions (Fig. 21). There is clearly no gatehouse as such: the outer enclosure wall which appears to be some 9 feet high is doubled in height to accommodate a large round-arched gateway with a postern beside it. A low brick shed stands outside the gate; within, behind the wall and apparently butting against it, are double storey buildings on each side of the gate. The age of the construction is difficult to judge. The brickwork has an inset diamond pattern which looks Tudor. This may be the original monastery gateway, or it may date from lay occupation. But it is clearly not the

Fig. 21 The gateway of Sheen, c1770. From a watercolour by Hieronymus Grimm (1733-94) in the Museum of Richmond. (Reproduced with permission of the Libraries Department of the Council of Richmond upon Thames.)

tower of Wyngaerde's drawing. This shows two faces of the tower which must be the south and east sides; the great vaulted arch is in the east face, wrongly aligned for a gate into Crown Court. Moreover the tower appears to stand at or about the eastern end of the monastery buildings, and to be surrounded by a number of lower buildings to south and west. The location and alignment are both appropriate for the church tower itself.

There is a quite striking resemblance between this tower with its vaulted archway as depicted by Wyngaerde and the ruined church tower of Mount Grace as depicted either in modern photographs or old prints.[106] The arch in the Mount Grace sketch (Fig. 22) is the tower arch revealed by the demolition of the chancel. This I believe is also what we see in the Wyngaerde drawing: the arch, on the east-west axis, is explained by this interpretation; most of the surrounding buildings can thereby be directly related to those whose existence we have already postulated. From right to left, starting by the tower, we may have first the reclusory in the foreground, with part of a chapel behind, adjacent to the tower. The tall building on the left of the tower could be part of the church itself; in front of it some of the outbuildings of the Prior's Lodging, whose gable end comes next. To the left of this, the buildings may be those on the south and west sides of the court housing the lay brothers, guest houses, etc. The tower itself looks more solid than that of Mount Grace, but this is to be expected with the larger church. I suggest then that the rebuilt chancel of 1556 was promptly pulled down again after the second Dissolution and had disappeared by 1562; the church tower, standing as at Mount Grace at the junction of nave and chancel, survived to be drawn by Wyngaerde and to be mentioned in the 1583 grant, but was taken down before 1635. A possible confirmation of this may be seen in the inventory of lands taken in 1551, where 'a parcel of land lying on the east of the Tower containing by estimation half an acre' is listed. A tower at the east end would be very odd. It is more likely that part of this open land was the site of the original chancel, shortly to be rebuilt and then destroyed again within a decade.

The overall length of the southern side of the Marian refoundation cloister is a little under 300 ft. The church probably occupied most of it, though its west end would probably have been on a line with the cloister walk rather than that of the outer walls. This might give us a total length for the church of, say, some 230 ft. We know that the nave was about 105 ft in length, so we may postulate that the tower stood in the centre, to the south of the chapter house. This gives us a plan for the church somewhat similar to that at Mount Grace, but on double the scale. The closeness in the date of construction of these two houses make such a similarity of design as probable as the difference in size of the foundations makes the difference of scale of the buildings. The large nave at Sheen may have been intended to accommodate the lay brothers; even when they had their own chapel in the 'lower house', they were required to attend some services in the main church.

We have now the completed plan E (see Fig. 23), showing the buildings of 1635-1649 and directly relatable to the Glover drawing, and can simply construct from it Plan F (Fig. 24) with the monastic buildings of the Marian refoundation. It remains to consider the great cloister of the original foundation. The northern wall is firmly fixed as the boundary wall of the site; the south is fixed by the church; we can assume that the west was on the same line as the Marian buildings; we have suggested above that the eastern outer enclosure may be on the line of the wall shown in the 18th century maps. Around the west, north and east sides of this court we can reasonably place some 24 cells with approximately 45 to 50 ft gardens. Three more cells at the east end of the south side and the three others to the north and south-west sides of the church for the Prior,

Fig. 22 Sketch of the tower of Mount Grace Priory from the south-east, by the author, 1975.

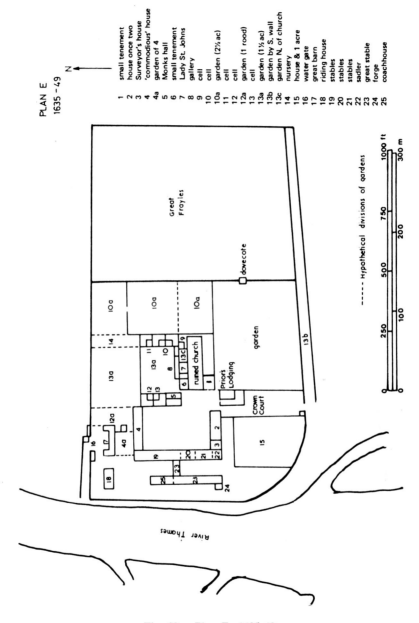

Fig. 23   Plan E: 1635-49.

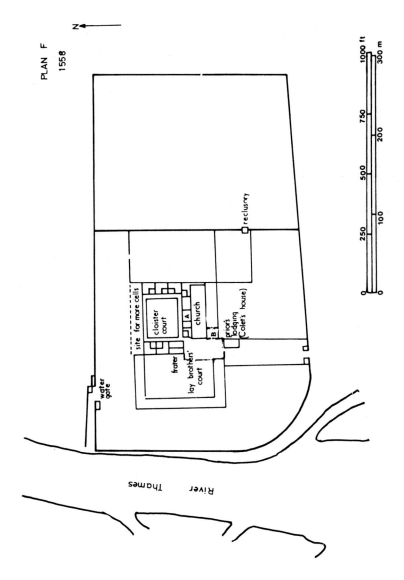

Fig. 24   Plan F: 1558 (A—Chapter House) (B—Procurator)

Sacrist and Procurator would give us the 30 we expect from William of Worcester's account.

We have no means of reconstructing the lay brothers' quarters and outer courts of the original foundation from documentary evidence, but it is of interest that the bequest of 1000 marks in Henry V's will was 'for the building of their greater house (ad aedificationem majoris domus suae)'[107] which rather suggests that the monastery may have followed to some extent the older Carthusian pattern of lower and upper houses for lay brothers and choir-monks respectively: and on this hypothesis the large western court seen in Moses Glover's drawing may well be the lay brothers' court, later converted into stables. It is likely that these stables would have used remaining parts, or at least foundations, of earlier buildings and the westernmost group of buildings in the Wyngaerde drawing (including one large one standing a full storey higher than its neighbours, which might be the guest house) seems to be well over towards the river.

The original line of the river bank was most likely well to the east of its present position. The meadows seem to 'grow' in the various inventories—land was probably reclaimed more than once from the river. There were aits 'by the Sheen wall'—both to the north and the south—which later disappeared. This process could explain both why the east-west dimension of the monastery site is substantially greater than the 1305 ft of the original grant, and why that outer western wall in Moses Glover's drawing has a sweeping curve at the southern end. Perhaps the first enclosure of extra ground followed the then course of the river bank; and the extra ranges of stabling were built on this reclaimed land.

And so we finally arrive at Plan G (Fig. 25)—a conjectural layout of the Charterhouse in its heyday, related to the map of today.

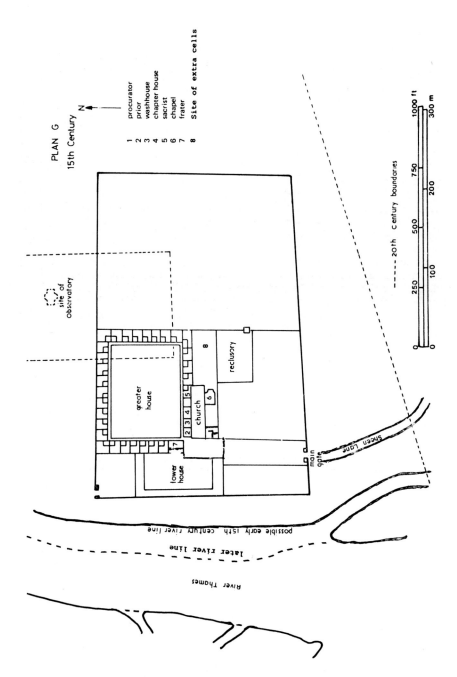

Fig. 25   Plan G: 15th century.

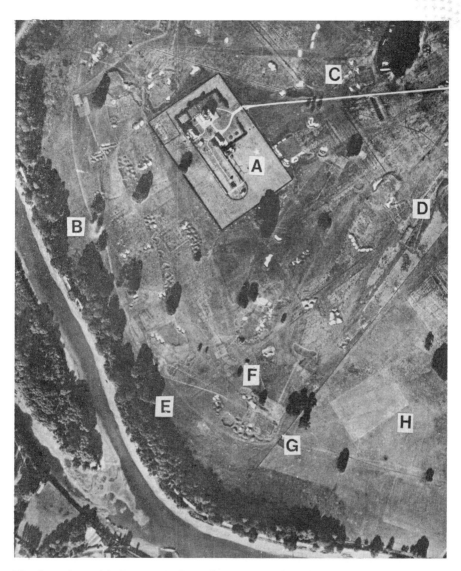

Fig. 26 An aerial photograph of the Charterhouse site, taken on 9 September 1929 at 3.50 p.m. The large rectangular enclosure is the Observatory and its attached ground (A). The corners of the monastery site are indicated by the letters B, C, D, E. The Crown Gate was at F and Sheen Lane ran from F by G and H to the north corner of Richmond Green. Compare Plan A (Fig. 14, p.26). (Richmond Public Library)

ARCHAEOLOGICAL EVIDENCE FROM THE SITE

No serious excavation work has been carried out on the Charterhouse site. However, the location of some walls and ditches which survived into the eighteenth century (some of which were undoubtedly of much older origin) can be clearly seen on the ground after a dry summer, revealed as long straight parch marks or as lines of unusual greenness.

An aerial photograph (Fig. 26) taken sixty years ago, in September 1929, shows almost every wall line that was drawn on the 1771 map, as well as some other easily disinguishable features such as the old lanes, including the former 'Sheen Lane' running from the Green to the Crown Court gate, and the grove which was planted outside the eastern wall of the West Sheen enclosure. Although what may be traces of the eighteenth century buildings can also be seen, the surface pattern of the Royal Mid-Surrey golf course, with its tees, fairways, bunkers and greens, makes it hard to identify any clear outlines of buildings other than the walls enclosing and dividing the site.

One early attempt at excavation was inadequately recorded and too rapidly abandoned. Richard Crisp, the mid-nineteenth-century historian of Richmond, was convinced that there should have been an underground passage beneath the river linking the monasteries of Shene and Syon. (This seems extremely unlikely!) In the winter of 1862-63, after some earth gave way exposing a kind of vault, he obtained permission to excavate. He uncovered 'a strongly built brick erection, 14 feet in length, 3 feet 2 inches in width and 6 feet high, slightly on the curve', built of old, thin bricks and with an arched brick roof. He was then stopped by a piece of more modern wall built across this passage, and abandoned the dig, intending to return. He delayed his return, and the tenant of the land, considering the excavation to be a hazard to cattle, had it refilled with earth. Crisp concluded that 'it was merely part of an underground passage from one part to another of the building which had formely stood over it'.[108] (The direction in which it was turning convinced him that it was not a tunnel under the river.[109]) He gave no indication of where exactly this passage was found. Although the existence of an underground pedestrian passage within the monastery is not impossible, a much more probable explanation is that such work would be a sewer, linked to the drains around the monastic premises. Consideration of the monastery plan shows that there were certainly some areas where these drains would have had to be carried underneath buildings; and as the drains would have been flushed by the rise and fall of the river, a considerable height would have been necessary in any such underground section.

There have been a few chance finds of stones and other traces of buildings, mostly exposed in the course of works on the golf course or at the Observatory. They were, unfortunately, very poorly recorded.

In 1893 a builder working at the Observatory found 'a passage 5' 6" high and 9' 9" wide' in the Observatory grounds, and also some foundation walls and tiled floors in the 'paddock' south of the Observatory enclosure—now a practice area for the golf course. These finds were plotted, at least roughly (See Fig. 27). It seems possible that the three parallel features may represent the lines of the cloister enclosure, including the area east of the church where the extra cells were probably added in 1457. The tiled floors might have come from the church

Fig. 27 Finds made in 1893. The finds made in the Paddock in 1893 when a local firm of builders, Jarmans, was doing some work at Kew Observatory were recorded on a plan. That plan cannot now be traced, but the diagram here, allegedly based on it, was drawn by a *Richmond and Twickenham Times* artist in 1956 to illustrate an article on the Charterhouse by Margaret G. Aldred. Its relationship to the Observatory site can be seen below. The Paddock is now the practice area.

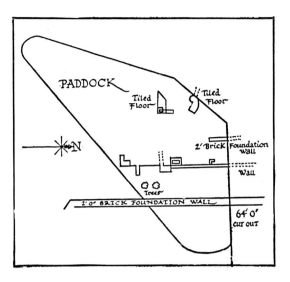

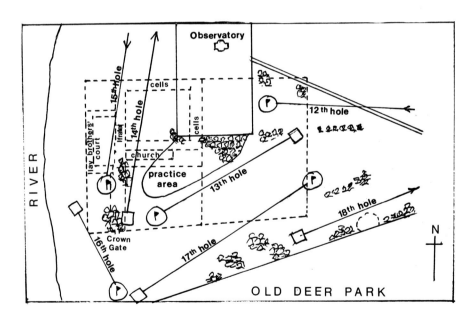

Fig. 28 The relationship of the Charterhouse plan to the present layout of the Royal Mid Surrey golf course. (The practice area south of the Observatory compound is the 'paddock' of the 1893 plan above.)

and the chapter-house, or might be the remains of later buildings. As there is no description of the tile-work, it is difficult to judge. These finds were said to have been 'bricked in'.

The next discovery seems to have been that of a Bellarmine jug (probably early 17th century) in 1924, but the location of this find (now in the Museum of Richmond) was not recorded.

Soon after this, a large section of 'intricately patterned stone mosaic work', measuring some 12 feet by 10 feet, was found 'under the turf of the 14th fairway' (but this is a long hole, so this location is very imprecise). A local archaeologist pronounced it to be 'part of the monastery floor'—and the 14th fairway does indeed cross the site of the church. This find was on public show for a few weeks; it was subsequently removed; its disposal is not recorded.[110]

The largest find, in 1929, of some hundred fragments of stone, many of which had some traces of carving, was briefly noted in the *Surrey Archaeological Collections* (vol. 38, p. 105), but the location of the find was not stated, and only one stone was drawn and published. Eighteen of the stones, which had been kept in the Richmond Public Library, were sent in 1967 to St Hugh's Charterhouse at Parkminster, near Partridge Green in Sussex. Four or five were photographed at that time. At St Hugh's they still remain, save for one stone which was sent on to the new charterhouse being built in Vermont, USA, and another which has been recovered for display in the Museum of Richmond. Most are badly deteriorated, and many are now very crumbly. The most interesting have however now been measured and photographed. Three appear to have come from a window arcade; the others are from various arches and vaults.

In 1935 some other stones (probably from later buildings) were found on the north and south sides of the 15th green; and were disposed in the car parking area of the old clubhouse. It is believed that one of these was a large block of masonry carved with the arms of Lord Bellasys which may come from a 17th century gateway, and which is now held by the Libraries Department of the Richmond upon Thames Council.

About 1950 a brick arch was discovered on the 8th fairway, and a drain on the 7th fairway. Though conceivably connected with the monastery's drainage system, these were more probably the relics of garden or farm works of Richmond Lodge. Another 'hole' which appeared on the course in 1969, and which revealed brickwork of a definitely post-Tudor date, was most likely part of the cellars of one of the 17th century mansions of West Sheen.[111] Although the vaults under the Observatory have been thought by some to be connected with the monastic buildings, they are too far from the monastery site to have had any such origin.

However, the great cloister of the Charterhouse did extend into the southwestern quarter of the ground now attached to the Observatory. In 1983 magnetometer and resistivity tests were carried out in this area. Although the anomalies found were far from conclusive, they did produce suggestive patterns of straight lines and rectangles in the very places where, if the reconstructed plans in this paper are correct, the cloister walls and some of the monks' cells would once have stood.[112]

Fig. 29   Stones of Shene.

    Above—stones from a window arcade.
    Bottom left—possibly from the upper part of a window or door arch.
    Bottom right—the springing of an arch (now in the Museum of Richmond).

        Photographs by the author, taken at St Hugh's Charterhouse, Parkminster.

The site of the Charterhouse as it is today.

Fig. 30 (above) General view, from the S.E.

Fig. 31 (below) Looking north-east from Crown Gate.

The site of the Charterhouse as it is today.
Fig. 32 (above) The site of the church, looking west.
Fig. 33 (below) The King's Observatory.

APPENDIX 1

AGREEMENT BETWEEN SIR JOHN BUCKWORTH AND JOHN JEFFREYS TO EXCHANGE HOLDINGS ETC. FOR THEIR MUTUAL CONVENIENCE—1702

The following is a summary of the signed copy at PRO (CRES 2/1241).

The agreement is dated 30 December 1702, but the document was formalised and witnessed 14 April 1703.

I   Buckworth assigns to Jeffreys:

    (i) kitchen garden of Sir John Buckworth as now walled and planted containing 215 rods and 100 feet, abutting on Mr Jeffreys' yard called Crown Court on the east, on the way from Richmond Lane to the Thames on the south, on the backyard of Sir John Buckworth on the west and on Mr Jeffreys' stables on the north (see C on plan); and the wall wherewith it is encompassed.

```
                    Buckworth backyard
                           290
                    ┌─────────────────┐
      Way from      │        C        │
      Richmond      │ Sir J. Buckworth's│   Mr Jeffreys'
      Lane to   202 │  Kitchen Garden │    stables
      the River     │                 │
                    │   215 r 100 ft  │
                    └─────────────────┘
                       Crown Court
```

    (ii) square piece of ground in Sir John Buckworth's yard, now or late Sir John Buckworth's drying yard, to range from the corner of the barn there to the said kitchen garden wall, as the same is now walled in (D on plan)

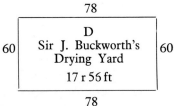

    (iii) liberty to and from the little farmhouse at the gate at the end of the lane from Richmond to Sheen.

    (iv) liberty to make if he wished his own water stairs to the Thames if he does not prejudice the watering places.

(v) liberty for Mr Jeffreys to make and maintain a vista through the kitchen garden wall and another vista through the wall of Sir John Buckworth next the river, such vistas not to exceed 20 feet (and to be proof against high tides).

II Buckworth to have from Jeffreys:

(i) a part of Jeffrey's frayles, from the corner of his orchard wall in a line to the lower end of the ground as it is marked out and now planted, to be divided by a wall (A on plan).

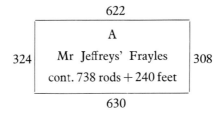

(ii) a piece of ground out of Lady Bellasys' backyard, from the corner of the little brick house at the end adjoining Lady Bellasys' house, to Sir John Buckworth's wall in a straight line (B on plan).

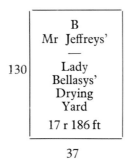

III Sir John Buckworth is to make a partition wall to divide the said ground (II ii) from the other part of the yard at his own charge, for which Sir John Buckworth is to have the said little brick house with the other old building at the end of the yard in the occupation of Sir John Buckworth, with all the materials thereof, and two elm trees thereon.

IV Mr Jeffreys is to make up the road with brick between Lady Bellasys' house and the little brick house.

V Sir John Buckworth releases all claim to a way or passage through Crown Court.

APPENDIX 2

ASSIGNMENT FROM PHILIP VISCOUNT LISLE TO JOHN LORD BELLASYS—12 DECEMBER 1661 (PRO: CRES 38/1765)

All that mansion or dwelling house where the said Viscount Lisle then lived in Sheen als West Sheen als Richmond, with the appurtenances, the front thereof abutting to the west and is built with stone and the east or back side thereof with brick,

— and the courtyard before the said house,

— and all that garden on the east side of the said house walled about with brick and coped with stone, together with the walls of the said garden,

— and all those outbuildings next adjoining unto the south end of the said mansion house, containing the kitchen, laundry, wash house and the new cellar and coal house near adjoining to it and whatsoever other rooms were contained in the said buildings,

— and all those two courtyards called the Laundry Court and the Kitchen Court both enclosed and separated from the said Viscount Lisle's other houses and courts there with two new brick walls, which said two new brick walls were to remain and be during the aforesaid term of three-score years as party walls equally between the said Viscount Lisle's and said Lord Bellasys' houses and are to be repaired at equal charge between them,

— and all that timber building thentofore used for coach houses and then appointed or intended for stables,

— and all that little piece of ground adjoining on the backside of the said coach houses or stables,

— and all that brick building called or known by the name of the painting house, adjacent to or upon the old wall next unto the Viscount Lisle's meadow called the Ferry Mead,

— and all that ground encompassed and enclosed with an ancient brick wall whereon the said mansion house and other the houses and buildings do stand as it was then abutted—beginning at the SE corner of the said Viscount Lisle's stables called the Green Stables next to the courtyard called the Crown Court going south, abutting east on the said Crown Court, unto the cross wall about thirty feet from the Great Gate entering into the said court, thence turning westward towards the River of Thames it abutteth south upon the way and foot path unto the Ferry, and from the SW corner of the said wall upon the waterside going northward abutteth west by the riverside and the aforesaid way, and from the NW corner of the said wall next the said Viscount Lisle's Ferry Mead near unto the Thames turning eastward abutteth on the aforesaid meadow in part and on the ground called Richmond Little Park in part on the north, which said wall from the NW corner near the Thames unto the partition wall next the said Viscount Lisle's grounds called the Great Frayles contains in length 53 perches and 14 feet of assize, and turning south abutteth east on the said grounds called Great Frayles unto the cross wall next the ground there in the possession of Master Wormall, and then turning westward abutteth south upon the last mentioned wall and the dwelling house of the said Master Wormall unto or near the said Viscount Lisle's building called Monks' Hall, and then turning northward abutteth west about 64 feet upon the said building called Monks' Hall, and abutting also south upon the said Viscount Lisle's other building and by the aforementioned new walls unto the NE corner of the aforesaid little piece of ground adjacent upon the coachhouses or stables abovementioned, and from the said coachhouses or stables, abutteth east on the said brick building called the Red Barn, and turning eastward by the SW corner of the Viscount Lisle's stables called the Green Stables, abutteth north on the said stables unto the Crown Court aforesaid where the boundary first began.

— and also the said ancient brick wall and other walls compassing or inclosing the said mansion house, buildings and other the premises aforesaid to be granted and assigned (except the two afore-mentioned brick walls), with all fruit trees . . .

— all which grounds inclosed as aforesaid contain by estimation 11 acres more or less,

— and all ways, paths and passages from the Ferry near adjoining to Richmond,

— and the liberty of water as it then ran in pipes to the premises,

— excepting only out of the said grounds, 32 feet of ground intended to be taken from that side where the said Master Wormall's house and the aforesaid wall standeth, and to be in length from the little garden on the side of the Monks' Hall aforesaid and reaching to the aforesaid wall of the Great Frayles for a passage to the said Frayles,

— excepting also another passage for coach or cart out of the said ground from the aforesaid Crown Court wall passing on the backside of the said Viscount Lisle's stables aforesaid into his stable yard, which passage to be 15 feet broad; which two passages or lanes to be separated by a sufficient brick wall to be built at the costs and charges of the said Viscount Lisle,

— all the said premises being part of the site of the Monastery of Sheen.

APPENDIX 3

SURVEY OF SHEEN MONASTERY, JANUARY 1649/50

The Parliamentary Survey was taken by Hugh Hindley Esq and others (PRO: E 317/Surrey 53)

1. Prior's Lodging (Mr Humphrey Parke)
   Fair and large structure called the Prior's Lodge containing a kitchen paved with freestone, a hall, a passage, a little parlour wainscotted, a great parlour wainscotted and a buttery, all floored with boards, one pantry room, two larders, one ground chamber, a porter's lodge and two cellars, one dining room, two bedchambers and withdrawing rooms and one closet all of them wainscotted and floored with boards and eight other chambers or rooms or large garrets all of them floored with boards; one great shed standing on the NW side of the Crown Court there, one dovecote, and one little shed for a stable, one great garden, outhouses within a large brick wall lying on the back side of the said building, well fitted and ordered for the growth of fruits, herbs, flowers and plants with 148 wall fruit trees, 317 trees of cherries and other fruits and one cypress tree, bordered with currant trees, gooseberry trees, little thorn hedges and some box borders; one little court before the door and one large court called the Crown Court; containing in the whole by estimate 5 acres of land worth p.a.   20.0.0

2. (Mr Humphrey Park)
   Small tenement between the last tenement and the south wall of the old church there, consisting of two ground rooms serving for a kitchen and a wash house and a gallery below stairs and two rooms above stairs with one little garden lying between the said last mentioned tenement and the said church wall containing in the whole by estimate about 10 perches, worth p.a.
                                                                                                     6.0.0

3. (Sir John Dingly)
   Tenement, part of stone and part of brick, formerly two tenements, one in the possession of John Hewson and the other in the occupation of John Knollys, consisting of 6 rooms below stairs and 7 rooms above stairs well ordered and fit worth p.a.   10.0.0

4. (Capt Jaques)
   Tenement of brick building containing three rooms below stairs and four rooms above stairs, heretofore in the occupation of one Palmer, late surveyor of the Prince's Stables, well ordered and fitted, worth p.a.   4.0.0

5. (George Pigot)
   Brick tenement with appurtenances, consisting of four rooms below stairs and 4 rooms above stairs, very commodious for a tenement; and one little garden lying at the SW end of the great barn there; containing by estimation 10 perches of land worth p.a.   5.0.0

6   Monks' Hall (Geo Pigot & Thos Barnes)
    Building of stone, containing two large cellars below stairs and one large room above stairs, formerly called the Monks' Hall, worth p.a.   0.10.0

7   (William Aynsway)
    Little tenement of brick building containing 3 rooms below stairs and 2 rooms above stairs worth p.a.   4.0.0

8   Lady St John's Lodging (George Cooke)
    Tenement, part of stone and part of brick, consisting of one room below and 4 rooms above, formerly called Lady St John's Lodging, with one little garden plot lying to the north wall of the said old church, worth p.a.   2.0.0

9   The Gallery (Widow Murray)
    Parcel of building called the Gallery adjoining to the last mentioned tenement on the south, part thereof wainscotted and floored with boards and now divided into three rooms, worth p.a.   2.0.0

10 Cell (Henry Heath)
    Tenement built of brick, heretofore used as an Anchorite's Cell, containing 2 rooms below and 2 above stairs, a long shed and a little garden, worth p.a.   4.0.0

11 Cell (Anthony Tilman)
    Tenement built with brick, heretofore used as an Anchorite's Cell, containing 4 rooms below and 4 above and two little gardens and one other garden being part of the old churchyard there, all well planted and ordered; containing in the whole by estimate 2 acres and 2 roods worth p.a.   8.10.0

12 Cell (Void of a tenant)
    Tenement built with brick heretofore used as an Anchorite's Cell, containing 2 rooms below and 2 rooms above stairs, a long shed and a little garden, worth p.a.   4.0.0

13 Cell (William Wood)
    Tenement built with brick heretofore used as an Anchorite's Cell, containing 2 rooms below and 2 above, 2 long sheds and a little outhouse used for a stable or cowhouse, and one rood of ground part of the aforesaid old churchyard, lying to the east side of the said great barn worth p.a.   5.0.0

14 Cell (Giles Hill)
    Tenement or Anchorite's Cell containing 2 rooms below and one above stairs, 3 little sheds, and one acre and a half of land part of the old churchyard aforesaid lying between the last mentioned parcel of land and one other parcel of the said churchyard used for a nursery; and one parcel of land adjoining to the south wall of the said late Monastery extending itself from the gate called the Crown Gate thirty and five feet in breadth to the end of the said wall, used for a garden; and also one other little piece of ground thirty feet broad adjoining to the north wall of the said church; containing in the whole $1\frac{1}{2}$ acres, worth   10.0.0

15 (John Fruen)
    Little tenement built with brick containing two rooms below and one shed and one great yard thereunto adjoining, lying between the said Crown Court and the Little Frayles or stable yard, containing by estimation one acre of land; and all that passage over the River of Thames called Shene Ferry (being only a passage for people on foot), worth   5.10.0

16 (Edward Watson)
Parcel of land lying in the old churchyard of Shene, and parcel thereof, now used and planted for a nursery, worth   1.10.0

17 Water Gate (no tenant)
Tenement called the back or water gate, containing two little rooms, worth   1.0.0

18 Great Barn
Great barn containing eleven bays of building, tiled on head and boarded on one side and two ends thereof, worth   3.10.0

19 Riding House
One other barn heretofore used for riding of the King's Great Horses, containing five bays of building, well tiled and ordered, worth   2.0.0

20 Stable for Great Horses
Range of brick building containing a large stable paved with free stone, posted, planked and well ordered and fitted for 16 great horses to stand abreast, well ceiled and tiled on head, worth   1.10.0

21 Hunting Stable
Range of brick building containing one double stable for six horses to stand abreast called the Hunting Stable, well paved planked and ordered, having a room over it for the laying of hay, one other room in the south end thereof, and

22 Coach Horse Stable
One other double stable ordered as aforesaid for six horses to stand abreast called the Coach Horse Stable, worth   1.0.0

23 Sadler's Office
Brick building adjoining the south end of the said Coach Horse Stable, containing one room below and three rooms above called the Sadler's Office, worth   1.0.0

24 Great Stable
One other fair range of brick building called the Great Stable, containing one large double stable, well paved, planked, posted and fitted for 12 horses to stand abreast; and one other stable ordered for 6 horses to stand abreast; over which two stables are two great and large granary rooms fitted for keeping of corn, well ceiled and tiled, worth   2.10.0

25 Coach House
One other parcel or range of building, part brick and part wood, adjoining the north end of the great stable, containing a large coach house below stairs and one granary room and 3 chambers or lodgings above stairs, well ceiled and tiled, worth   1.10.0

26 Smith's Forge
Brick building adjoining the S. end of the Great Stable building, called the Smith's Forge, containing a room ordered for a smith's forge, one other ground room, and one room overhead, worth   1.0.0

27 Little Frayles
Parcel of land called the Little Frayles or Stable Yard, upon part whereof the said barns and stables before mentioned do stand and containing by estimate 4 acres more or less, worth   4.0.0

28 Great Frayles (William Wood)
Parcel of land or meadow ground enclosed round with a brick wall commonly called the Great Frayles, lying between the tenements last mentioned and Richmond Little Park, containing by estimation 10 acres more or less, worth   15.0.0

29 Dovecote (William Wood)
Dovecote standing in and upon the said close or parcel of meadow called the Great Frayles worth   0.5.0

30 Great Meadow (George Pigot)
Parcel of lands or meadow ground formerly belonging to the said Monastery of Shene commonly called the Great Meadow, lying between the said Little Park of Richmond and the River of Thames, and extending itself from the south wall of the said late Monastery unto the crane at Richmond Palace, containing upon admeasurement 27 ac, 1 rood, 3 perches worth   54.0.0

31 Lower Meadow (George Pigot & Thos Barnes)
Parcel of meadow ground formerly belonging to the said late Monastery of Shene commonly called the Lower Meadow, lying between the said Little Park and the said River of Thames, adjoining to the north wall of the said late Monastery, containing upon admeasurement 15 ac, 2 roods, 20 perches, worth   30.0.0

And all ways, passages . . . etc . . . etc.

Memo: That all the said messuages or tenements, lands or premises before mentioned, except the 2 meadows called the Great Meadow and the Lower Meadow, are enclosed within a brick wall of 12 feet high, severing the same from the said Little Park of Richmond. The premises enclosed by the said brick wall do contain upon admeasurement 32 ac, 2 roods, 2 perches, the yearly value of all which area herein before particularly mentioned.

Memo: The tenements before mentioned are very well accommodated with water which is brought and conveyed unto them through several small pipes of lead branched from one great pipe of lead from the stopcock or conduit head on Richmond Green unto a great cistern of stone placed within the said wall of Shene.

The said several tenements, barns, stables, dovecotes and other buildings before mentioned are in good tenantable repair and not fit to be demolished yet we have taken a full view of the same together with the materials thereof and we do estimate the same to be worth in the timber, leads, tiles, bricks, stone, glass, iron and lead in pipes and otherwise upon the place, besides the charge of taking down the same £1149-17-4

Memo: There is a part of the old Church of Shene yet standing but very ruinous and fit for nothing but to be demolished and taken down, the materials whereof besides the charge of taking down the same are worth £10-0-0

The brick walls in and about the said Monastery of Shene are very large and spacious and are a great ornament and of special use . . . the materials whereof besides the charge of taking down the same are worth £150-0-0

And then the site of the said late Priory or Monastery of Shene containing 32 acres, when the said materials are cleared is value to be worth p.a.
£32-0-0

There are 322 pollard trees standing and growing upon the premises, being good for little save for the fire, we estimate to be worth upon the place (the time of converting them into money considered) £64-8-0

* * *

Note: The additional passages below are taken from the sale particulars (E 320/R23)

Memorandum It is certified by the Survey that the aforesaid were by Letters Patent dated the second of May 1638 demised to James Duke of Lenox for the term of his natural life at the yearly rent of three pounds six shillings and eight pence.

Memorandum It is certified upon information that all the lands belonging the late dissolved Priory of Shene are tithe free and have never been charged with the payment of any tithes.

Memorandum It is found upon enquiry that the Stables called the stables for the Great horse the stables called the hunting stables and coach horse stable with the saddlers office in the south end thereof the great stables with the two granaries over the same the said coach house room and the granary room and the three chambers over the coach house and the smith's forge and the two rooms aforementioned belonging thereunto the great barn and the other barn used for riding of the great horse, the aforementioned tenement containing six rooms in the occupation of George Piggott and the said parcel of land called the Little Frayles whereon all the premises last mentioned do stand were reserved for the use of the late King for his stables and outhouses belonging to the Palace of Richmond and that the Duke of Lenox did never intermeddle therein or let, sell or dispose of the same as he did of other the premises.

And it is further certified by the Survey that the surveyors are informed that the said Duke is to yield to the Chief Keeper at Richmond Little Park yearly fifteen cartloads of hay forth of the said Sheene meadows.

. . . .

The improved yearly rent of the premises over and above the rent reserved is £207-18-04

APPENDIX 4

THE OTHER MONASTIC HOUSES OF RICHMOND

I. THE CARMELITE FRIARY (1315-1318)

According to a contemporary account,[113] King Edward II, when fleeing for his life after his defeat by the Scots at Bannockburn in June 1314, vowed that if he escaped he would found a new house for Carmelite Friars. (The Carmelites were known as 'White Friars' from the colour of their habits.) He honoured his pledge by establishing twenty-four Carmelites in his manor house at Shene. The buildings were adapted for their use in 1314-15,[114] and in December 1315 he granted them 120 marks 'for their sustenance'.[115] In the following July he granted them the manor house in perpetuity.[116]

However, the King then found what he considered a better home for them. On 1 February 1317/8 he gave them part of the old royal house called Beaumont, just outside the north gate of Oxford.[117] He must have moved them at once, for they appear to have been already established at Oxford when he renewed his maintenance grant on 10 February.[118] Their church at Shene was demolished,[119] and the manor house reverted to royal use.

II. THE OBSERVANT (FRANCISCAN) FRIARY (1501-1534)

The 'Grey Friars' of the Franciscan order had been reformed in 1421, but some houses of the order resisted the reforms. The reformed houses were called 'Observant'; the non-reformed 'Conventual'.

King Henry VII was a strong supporter of the Observants. He suppressed four houses of Conventuals and handed them over, with the Pope's blessing, to the Observants. About 1501 he followed an example set by Edward IV, who had set up an Observant Friary in part of the Greenwich Palace buildings in 1482, by himself founding a new house of Observants at Richmond Palace.

The King had just completed the rebuilding of the palace, severely damaged by fire in December 1497, and had celebrated the event by renaming the palace 'Richmond' (from his Yorkshire earldom) instead of Shene. During the rebuilding he had probably been using the old 'Byfleet' buildings adjacent to the palace, and these were now vacant and available for the Friars. (They were called 'Byfleet' because Henry V had re-erected at Shene the royal manor house formerly at Byfleet to provide temporary accommodation while he made a start on his rebuilding of Shene Palace, destroyed by order of Richard II.)

There is no foundation charter, but work on converting the buildings for the Friars' use must have started late in 1501 or early in 1502, as the first payment on the contract was made in May 1502.[120] Payments continued fairly regularly until July 1507; then there was a final one in March 1509 to the Clerk of the King's Works 'for full fynysshing of the Freres at Richmond'.[121]

The Friary was separated from the Palace by a narrow lane (now Friars Lane), spanned by a covered bridge which gave direct access from the galleries around the Palace gardens into the Friars' chapel. The northern boundary of the site was behind the buildings that now line King Street and the southern corner of the Green. (The house called 'Old Friars' was outside the site.) On the east the ground stretched almost to Water Lane; on the south the boundary wall near the riverside was approximately where the high brick wall on the north side of the open car park now stands.

There was a close association between the Palace and the Friary. Both from Greenwich and from Richmond the Observant Friars provided preachers and confessors for the royal family. Henry VIII's short-lived firstborn son by Catherine of Aragon was baptized in the Richmond Friary chapel on 5 January 1510/1.[122] But when, some seventeen years later, the issue of the validity of the King's marriage became public knowledge, the Observants were prominent in their opposition to the idea of divorce or annulment. The Friars at Canterbury and at Richmond were strong supporters of the 'Nun of Kent', whose preaching and prophesying against the divorce provided a focus for the opposition. When the Nun finally confessed to fraud in her prophecies in 1533, Dr Hugh Rich, who was almost certainly the Warden of the Richmond Friary,[123] was one of those arrested. Rich appears to have died in prison; the Nun and her supporters were hanged for treason.

The opposition of the Observant Friars was seen by the Chancellor, Thomas Cromwell, as particularly dangerous because of their closeness to the royal family, because their ranks included many leading theologians, and—above all—because they were itinerant preachers. The Friars of Richmond and Greenwich became his prime target for forced submission. They remained adamant, however, in their refusal to take the oath accepting the Act of Succession which declared Henry's marriage with Catherine to be void.[124] In the summer of 1534 the entire order in England was suppressed, the monks were expelled from their houses (seven in all) and most were imprisoned in the Tower of London or in other monastic houses—although a few managed to escape abroad.[125]

Queen Mary restored the Observant Friars at Greenwich, and was reported to be intending to restore also the Richmond house.[126] But the Friary at Richmond was never again occupied as such. Its chapel survived to be drawn by Wyngaerde in 1562, though it was by then in considerable disrepair; but by the 1560s, if not earlier, the site of the Friary was granted out on lease to residents of the town.[127] A part in the corner adjacent to the house now called 'Old Friars' became an extension to that house's garden. The rest was usually leased to the owner of the three houses (later joined into one) that became 'Old Palace Place'. One of these, a London alderman named William Bolton, built a house at the eastern end of the site during the Commonwealth.[128]

Later, when extra ground by the riverside, reclaimed in the early seventeeth century, had been added to the site, stables and a brewery were built. In the 1760s the houses of Cholmondeley Walk were built, and Friars Lane—originally straight—was diverted around them. The first building of the White Cross Tavern was erected about 1768, followed in the 1770s by the row of cottages called White Cross Buildings (parallel with Water Lane—since demolished). Boat houses sprang up by the riverside.

In 1833 the whole site was finally sold off by the Crown in separate freehold lots. There followed the development of St Helena Terrace, Queensberry Villas, the Retreat and Retreat Road, etc.

Fig. 34 The chapel of the Friary at Richmond in 1562. Detail from a sketch by Antonis van den Wyngaerde. On the left are the galleries round the gardens of the Palace. The covered bridge over Friars Lane is linked to the tower in the middle of the galleries. By this date the chapel, originally part of the 'Byfleet' complex, was in considerable disrepair.

(Reproduced with permission of the Trustees of the Ashmolean Museum, Oxford.)

NOTES AND REFERENCES

ABBREVIATIONS USED
- BL — British Library
- PRO — Public Record Office

Secondary Sources

Deanesley *IA*	*The Incendium Amoris of Richard Rolle of Hampole* ed. M. Deanesley, 1915
Harvey *EMA*	Harvey, J., *English Mediaeval Architects, a biographical dictionary*, 1954
HKW	*History of the King's Works*, ed. H. M. Colvin (Vol. 2, 1963)
M and B	Manning, Rev Owen, and Bray, W., *History and Antiquities of Surrey*, 3 vols, 1804-14
Thompson *COE*	Thompson, E. M., *The Carthusian Order in England*, 1930

State Papers Calendars

CChR	*Calendar of Charter Rolls*
CLPFD	*Calendar of Letters and Papers, Foreign and Domestic, Henry VIII*
CPR	*Calendar of Patent Rolls*
CSP Dom	*Calendar of State Papers, Domestic*
CSP For	*Calendar of State Papers, Foreign*
CSP Spanish	*Calendar of State Papers, Spanish*
CSP Venetian	*Calendar of State Papers, Venetian*
CTB	*Calendar of Treasury Books*
SP Henry VIII	*State Papers of Henry VIII*

Classes of documents in the Public Record Office

CRES	Crown Estate Office
E	Exchequer
LR	Land Revenue Office
SC	Special Collections
T	Treasury

Notes (Volume numbers are shown in heavy type)

1. Deanesly *IA*, 91 sqq and Knowles, D. *The religious orders in England*, 1955, **2**, 175sqq are the main sources for the following paragraphs
2. Deanesly *IA*, 120
3. Deanesly *IA*, 114-27; Knowles, *op cit*, **2**, Appendix II
4. Deanesly *IA*, 95-105
5. *CChR* **5** 1341-1417, 469
6. *ibid*, 479. The text is given in Dugdale's *Monasticon*, **6**, 31-2
7. Rymer's *Foedera*, **9**, 290
8. *CPR* 1416-22, 114. See Deanesly *IA*, 116 and Thompson *COE*, 241

9   Thompson *COE*, 241
10 *CPR 1441-46*, 56. Grant of 20 March 1442: '64 acres of land parcels of Shene manor, lying between the road which leads from the said house [the Monastery] towards the site of the manor on the south and the water of Thames on the north, and adjoining the land of the Prior and monks on the west'.
11 *CPR 1476-85*, 156. Confirmation by King's letters patent dated 25 May 1479 of grant made by Queen Elizabeth on 1 April 1479: '48 acres of land in West Shene parcel of the said manor and lordship lying between the River of Thames on the north and the way leading towards le Breikhouse of West Shene on the south and between the land of the said Prior and monks on the west and the warren of Shene on the east, and enclosed with hedges and ditches'.
12 *CPR 1422-29*, 222; *CPR 1461-67*, 160-1; *CPR 1461-67*, 513; *CPR 1467-77*, 467; *CPR 1476-85*, 210; *CPR 1494-1509*, 510; *CLPFD*, **1i**, 174; *CLPFD*, **2i**, 107
13 The report in a letter to Lord Lisle dated 15 May 1534 (*CLPFD*, **7**, no 671), that the Priors of both the London and Shene Charterhouses were in the Tower, was evidently incorrect.
14 Thompson, *COE*, 436-40
15 *CSP Venetian*, **6i**, 651
16 The story of the re-foundation is given in Thompson *COE*, 500-9, and in Hendriks, Dom L. *The London Charterhouse*, 1889, 280sqq; both based on Chauncy's own account 'De reparatione Carthusianae religionis in Anglia et ejusdem denuo eliminatione' in the *Passio* of 1570
17 *CPR 1555-7*, 354-5
18 Hendriks, *op cit*, 281
19 Thompson *COE*, 501
20 *ibid*, 509
21 *ibid*, 510-1. A full account of the Sheen Aglorum community is given in Hendriks, *op cit*, 285-348. Their final home was at Nieuport, and the final dissolution that decreed by the Emperor Joseph II in 1783
22 *HKW*, **2**, 265; E364/58 rot G
23 *HKW* **2**, 265; Walter Walton was appointed on 26 November 1397 chief surveyor of all stone cutters and masons for the King's works in England. He worked on Westminster Hall with Yevele and also on Porchester Castle (Harvey *EMA*)
24 Thompson *COE*, 239. The foundation stone of Sion was laid by the King himself on 22 February 1415 (Deanesly *IA*, 105-6)
25 B.L. Add MS 24062 f145
26 Rymer's *Foedera* **9**, 290
27 *CPR 1416-22*, 87 and 141
28 Thompson *COE*, 240-1
29 *HKW* **2**, 265; E364/58 rot G (There is a misprint in *HKW*: 'Syon' should read 'Sheen')
30 *CPR 1416-22*, 445
31 *CPR 1416-22*, 397; E 364/58 rot G
32 Thompson *COE*, 240
33 Thompson *COE*, 240
34 Harvey, J. H. *William Worcestre Itineraries*, 1969, 270-1. Worcester also intended to give a dimension for the 'width' of the cloister (the distance between the outside wall and the cloister walk?), but never filled in the figure

35 *ibid,* xv and xvii. Harvey comments that there appears to be 'a progressive degree of inaccuracy in the longer measurements' (i.e. over 100 ft or so), but that 'when all is considered, his degree of accuracy over moderate distances was remarkably high'
36 For London Charterhouse and Mount Grace comparisons see pp.32-35
37 Thompson *COE,* 507
38 *CPR* 1461-7, 513
39 E 317 Surrey 53: Parliamentary Survey January 1649
40 *CLPFD* **3,** 1519-23, 105, no 303; letter dated 13 June 1519 from Erasmus to Jodocas Jonas
41 Boccatelli, L. *Life of Cardinal Reginald Pole,* 1766, 14, 20; Schenk, W. *Reginald Pole, Cardinal of England,* 1950, 19-23
42 Cavendish, G. *The Life and Death of Cardinal Wolsey,* ed. R. S. Sylvester, 1959, 130
43 Boccatelli, *op cit,* 23; Schenk, *op cit,* 25-29; *SP Henry VIII* **13i,** no 42
44 Thompson *COE,* 507-8
45 SC 6 Henry VIII 3464 m 53; Lands of dissolved monasteries: Sheen
46 *CLPFD* **16,** 1540-41, 381, no 779(7)
47 *CLPFD* **16,** 1540-41, 723, no 1500 (Aug Book 213 f 3b)
48 SC 6 Henry VIII 3464 m 53 and E318/572 f 15—Particular for grant to Earl of Hertford
49 E 305 G 33—Surrender by Edward Duke of Somerset to King Edward VI, 1 July 1 Edward VI. For grant of lands in exchange dated 16 July 1547 see *CPR* 1547-8, 172
50 LR2/190, 100. Survey dated 4 January 5 Edward VI
51 *Privy Council Acts* **1,** 452. Letter of 28 December 1551 to the Chancellor of Augmentations 'to make out a book (sic) to the Duke of Suffolk for the keeping of the King's Majesty's house at Sheen'.
52 M and B, **1,** 420
53 Chapman, Hester W. *Two Tudor portraits,* 1960, 167-8
54 Thompson *COE,* 504-5
55 Chapman, *op cit,* 183-4
56 *CSP For,* 1562, 83
57 *CSP Dom,* 1547-80, 318; Sackville-West, R. W. *Works of Thomas Sackville,* 1859, Appx II, xxix-xxxiii
58 E 310/25/142, 49. Particular and warrant for lease to Sir T. Gorges, 2 May 1584. Grant dated 23 June 1584 (Patent 26 Elizabeth p. 3). Manning says that the Priory was in the occupation of Percival Gunston Gent. in 1572, but I cannot trace any grant. However, Gunston received in 1572 a grant of part of the land at Richmond formerly occupied by the Convent of Observant Friars (*CPR* 1569-72, 331, no 2240) and this may have given rise to a misunderstanding.
59 *CSP Dom.* Elizabeth & James I, addenda, 462—Letter of King to Lord Treasurer dated 22 May 1605
60 Devon, F. *Issues of the Exchequer Reg James I,* 1836, 179, 210
61 Cited in E 214/314 and E 214/462 (indenture re land surrendered to the King)
62 E 214/314. Surrender by Viscount Belhaven dated 22 February 1638
63 Patent 14 Charles I, p. 43 (cited in Parliamentary Survey)
64 *CSP Dom.* Parliamentary Committee for Compounding. Pt 2, p. 1526
65 E 317/Surrey 53
66 Map of Isleworth Hundred by Moses Glover, 1635, belonging to the Duke of Northumberland—at Syon House, Isleworth

67 E 320/R 23. Particulars for Sale dated 17 April 1650, annotated in respect of contract of sale
68 *CSP Dom.* Charles II 1660-61, 140
69 *CSP Dom.* Charles II 1660-61, 208. (Terms of lease recited in abstract of title of John Jeffreys, CRES 2/1241, and in 1750 lease to Jeffreys E 376/4766)
70 CRES 38/1763. Text at Appendix 2
71 See abstract of title at CRES 2/1241
72 Warrant for grant: *CSP Dom.* Charles II 1661-62, 258 and 308. Lease dated 20 March 1661: CRES 2/1241 and E 367/4766
73 See CRES 2/1241 (abstract of title)
74 Woodbridge, H. E. *Sir William Temple: the man and his work*, 59. Temple had a pew allotted to him in Richmond Church in 1672 (*Richmond Notes*, no 33, Nov. 1865, 125)
75 Longe, J. G. *Martha Lady Giffard: her life and correspondence (1664-1722)*, 70
76 Woodbridge, *op cit*, 59(n) and 114; and Longe, *op cit*, 132 and 169
77 CRES 2/1241
78 *CSP Dom.* Charles II 1675-6, 177
79 Warrant for reversionary grant to Robert Raworth and Martin Folkes, 1 Oct 1675: *CTB* 4, 1672-75, 824-5. Lease dated 24 Nov 1675: CRES 2/1241, E 367/4766 and E 367/7214
80 CRES 2/1241 (abstract of title)
81 Evelyn, J. *Diary*, ed. E. S. de Beer, 1955, 4, 142
82 Longe, *op cit*, 168-71; also Woodbridge, *op cit*, 212-3
83 Woodbridge, *op cit*, 214-6
84 Evelyn's Diary, 4, 575
85 CRES 2/1241 (abstract of title)
86 *ibid*
87 Copy of agreement dated 30 December 1702 (formalized and witnessed 14 April 1703) among papers at CRES 2/1241. See summary at Appendix 1.
88 E 367/4766 (papers on 1750 lease to Jeffreys); CRES 2/1241 (papers on 1750 lease, 1764 sub-lease to Reeson, and on compensation for resumption of lease by Crown)
89 E 367/7214 (lease to Charles Buckworth)
90 Extract from old newspapers in Richmond Public Library. See also Harris, J. *Sir William Chambers*, 1970, 78-80
91 CRES 2/1241
92 The Wyngaerde drawings are in the Ashmolean Museum. The finished drawing from the river is reproduced in Dunbar, J. *Prospect of Richmond*, 1966, and in Cundall, H. M. *Bygone Richmond*, 1925. The latter also reproduces the rough sketch.
93 Copies of these plans are in the Richmond Public Library
94 Rocque, J., *An exact survey of the City's of London, Westminster . . . and the country near ten miles round*, 1746 (on 16 sheets) and *An exact plan of the Royal palace gardens and park at Richmond*, 1754. (This is the third edition; the two earlier, and larger-scale, ones show no details of the monastery site.)
95 *The Royal Gardens of Richmond and Kew with the hamlet of Kew, part of the Royal Manor of Richmond*, 1771, made under the direction of Peter Burrell, Esq., His Majesty's Surveyor General, by T. Richardson.

96 Squaring off the irregular western corners to form a near rectangle, the dimensions given (in feet) are: 1390 (north), 1370 (south main wall), 1120 (south outer wall), 551 (west), 512 (east, overall including the end of the strip enclosed by the south outer wall). The same dimensions, except the south outer wall, appear on a surveyor's note of 1765 at CRES 2/1241
97 CRES 2/1241
98 CRES 2/1241 (abstract of title)
99 CRES 38/1765
100 The following passages are derived from:
    Knowles, D. and Grimes, W. F. *Charterhouse*, 1954, 68-82
    Thompson *COE*, 167-98 and 229-38
    Yorkshire Archaeological Journal **18**, 1905, 241-309 (especially the article on the 'Architectural history of Mount Grace Charterhouse' by W. H. St John Hope, 270sqq, and the plan therewith)
    Dimensions are taken from the plans of the London and Mount Grace Charterhouse in the above. Plans are also to be found in:
        Cook, G. H. *English monasteries in the middle ages*, 1961
        Godfrey, W. H. *History of architecture in and around London*, 1962
        Phillips, A. *A look round the monasteries of North East Yorkshire*, 1962
    Dept. of the Environment, *Guide to Mount Grace Priory*, 1971
101 E 317/Surrey 53
102 E 310/25/142, 49
103 Thompson *COE*, 176
104 M and B, **1**, 422
105 There are in fact two versions of this drawing: a water colour in the collection belonging to the Corporation of Richmond upon Thames now on loan to the Museum of Richmond, and an ink and wash drawing in the Richmond Public Library, which appears to be either a sketch for or a copy from the water colour. Both are undated, but the water colour is identified as by Samuel Hieronymous Grimm (1733-94) and is thought to be c1770.
106 Compare, for example, the illustrations in Phillips, *op cit*
107 Rymer's *Foedera*, **9**, 290
108 Crisp, Richard, *Richmond and its Inhabitants*, 1866, 122-4
109 Letter from 'R.C.' in *Richmond Notes*, No 23, January 1865
110 The finds were summarized in a series of articles by Margaret Aldred in the *Richmond and Twickenham Times*, 17 and 31 December 1955, 18 and 24 August 1956. (Her attempted reconstruction of the plan of the Charterhouse in the 18 August article is totally inaccurate.) The diagram of the 1893 finds (Fig. 27) was published in the issue of 7 January 1956.
111 Copy of a letter from the Librarian to the Secretary of the Golf Club, 7 March 1969 (in the Richmond Public Library)
112 Ancient Monuments Laboratory Report: Geophysics 22/83
113 *Chronicles Edward I and Edward II* (Rolls Series II), 300
114 SC **6**/1014/3 m 2
115 *CPR* 1313-17, 377
116 *ibid*, 514
117 *CPR* 1317-21, 75
118 *ibid*, 103
119 SC 6/1014/6 m 2
120 E 101/415/3 f94v
121 E 36/214, f328

122 *CLPFD* **1i**, 370 (no 670)
123 Some writers have considered Dr Rich to be the Warden at the Canterbury Observants, but this was Dr Risby. Rich was certainly at Richmond in October 1533 and January 1533/4 (*CLPFD* **6**, 544, and **7**, 143)
124 *CLPFD* **7**, 242-3 (no 622) and 316 (no 841)
125 *ibid*, 320 (no 856), 413 (no 1057), 423-5 (no 1095)
126 *CSP Spanish* **13**, 146
127 *CPR* 1569-72, 331 (no 2440); C66/1082 m 14
128 T 51/6 f56; E 367/3648 (plan with 1698 grant)

INDEX

Aldred, Margaret G.   51, 72
Alnwick, William, recluse   7
Andrews, Mr   23
Anne (of Bohemia), Queen   7
Ashburnham, Earl of   23
Aynsway, William   61

Bannockburn, battle of   65
Barnes, Thomas   61, 63
Beaufort, Henry, Bishop of Winchester   10
Beaumont House, Oxford   65
Belhaven, Lord *see* Douglas, Robert
Bellarmine jug   52
Bellasys (Belasyse), John, Lord   19, 21, 28, 41, 52, 58
Bellasys (Belasyse), Lady   28, 31, 57
Blundell, Lord   23
Bolton, Alderman William   66
Brigittine order   7
Brounker, Henry, Viscount   21, 23
Bruges   9
Bruno, Saint   7
Buckhurst, Lord *see* Sackville, Thomas
Buckworth, Charles   23, 25
Buckworth, Lt. Francis   23
Buckworth, Sir John, Bt.   23, 25, 28, 31, 39, 56-7
'Byfleet' building at Shene   65

Caen, Normandy   10
Calico printing   23
Canterbury, Kent   66
Carmelite Friary of Shene   65
Carthusian order   7, 9
     Central Chapter   10
     monasteries   7, 31-2, 47
     (*see also* Charterhouses)
     monk's habit   6
Cary, Elizabeth   23
Cary, Walter   23
'Cary-Reeson house'   23-4, 28, 36
Catherine (of Aragon), Queen   66
Cavendish, George   12
Celestine order   7
Chambers, Sir William   23
Charterhouses, Bruges   9
     Grande Chartreuse   7, 9
     London   9, 12, 32, 35, 37, 41, 69
     Mount Grace   10, 12, 32, 33, 35, 37, 43, 44
     St Hugh's, Parkminster   6, 52
     Sheen Anglorum   9, 69
Charterhouse of Shene
     foundation   7-8
     building works   10-13
     materials   10, 15, 53, 63
     surrender   9
     refoundation   9, 13
     second dissolution   9
     model   5, 13
     chapterhouse of   37, 46, 52
     church of   36, 37, 41, 51, 54, 60-1, 63
Chatillon, Cardinal de   15
Chatrousse, France   7
Chauncy, Maurice, Prior of Shene   9, 12, 36, 38-9
Cholmondeley Walk, Richmond   66
Colet, John, Dean of St Paul's   11, 12, 36
Coligny, Admiral   15
Conventual friars   65
Cooke, George   61
Crisp, Richard   50
Crofts, William, Lord   19, 28, 31
Cromwell, Thomas, Earl of Essex   66
Crown Court   21, 23, 28, 31, 35-6, 38 9, 41, 50, 56, 58-9, 60-1
Crown Gate   28, 31, 38, 41-2, 49-50, 54, 61

Darnley, Earl of *see* Stewart, Henry
Dingly, Sir John   60
Dorset, Earl of *see* Sackville, Thomas
Douglas, Sir Robert, Lord Belhaven   19
Dovecotes   41, 63
Dudley, Guildford   15
Dudley, Jane *see* Grey, Jane
Dudley, John, Earl of Warwick, Duke of Northumberland   15

Eaton, Alexander   19
Edward II, King of England   65
Edward IV, King of England   9, 10, 12, 65, 69
Edward VI, King of England   15
Elizabeth (Widville), Queen   9, 69
Elizabeth I, Queen of England   5, 9, 15, 19, 35
Eric XIII, King of Sweden   7
Evelyn, John   21, 23, 41

Ferry (Shene or Isleworth)   59, 61
Ferry Mead   58
Fishbourne, Thomas, recluse   7
FitzHugh, Henry, Baron Ravensworth   7
'Flesshehall'   41
Folkes, Martin   71
Franciscan order   65
Frayles, Great   25, 28, 41, 57, 59, 63
Frayles, Little   39, 61, 62
Friars Lane, Richmond   65-7
Friary, Richmond *see* Observant
Friary, Shene *see* Carmelite
Fruen, John   61

General Chapter *see* Carthusian order	
George III, King of England	23
Glover, Moses	19, 25, 31, 34, 36-9, 41, 43, 47
Gorges, Sir Thomas	15, 18, 31, 35, 41
Grande Chartreuse *see* Charterhouses	
Great Barn	36, 39, 62, 64
Great Meadow	63
Green Stables	28, 31, 58, 59
Greffier, Jan	22, 25
Gregory XII, Pope	7
Greenwich Friary	65, 66
Greenwich Palace	65
Grey, Frances, Duchess of Suffolk	15
Grey, Henry, Duke of Suffolk	9, 14, 15
Grey, Lady Jane	15
Grey, Lady Katherine	15
Grey, Lady Mary	15
Grimes, W. F.	35
Grimm, Samuel Hieronymous	42, 72
Gunston, Percival	70
Harvey, John	12, 70
Heath, Henry	61
Henry IV, King of England	7
Henry V, King of England	7, 8, 10, 47, 65
Henry VI, King of England	9
Henry VII, King of England	9, 65
Henry VIII, King of England	9, 15, 66
Henry, Prince of Wales	19
Hertford, Earl of, *see* Seymour, Edward	
Hertishorne, John	10
Hewson, John	60
Hill, Giles	61
Hillesdenwell	12
Hindley, Hugh	60
Hinton, Cambs.	7
Hunter, James	23
Isleworth	15, 34, 40
James IV, King of Scotland	15
James VI, King of Scotland, and I of England	19
Jane (Seymour), Queen	15
Jaques, Capt.	60
Jarmans, builders	51
Jeffreys, John I	23, 25, 39, 56-7
II	23, 24, 25, 35
Kent, Nun of (Elizabeth Barton)	66
Kew Palace ('White House')	24
King Street, Richmond	65
Knollys, John	60
Knowles, Prof. Dom David	35
Lady St John's lodging	37, 61
Leicester, Earl of *see* Sidney, Philip	
Lennox, Duke of *see* Stewart, James	
Lennox, Earl of *see* Stewart, Matthew	
Lennox, Margaret, Countess of *see* Stewart, Margaret	
Lisle, Viscount *see* Sidney, Philip	
London Charterhouse *see* Charterhouses	
Long, Mr	23
Lote, Stephen	10
Lower Meadow	63
Lyttleton, Sir Charles	21, 23
Manning, Rev Owen	41
Mary I, Queen of England	5, 9, 15, 66
Materials for building	10, 15, 53, 63
Monks' hall	28, 31, 35, 37, 59, 61
Moor Park, Farnham	21
Mount Grace Charterhouse *see* Charterhouses	
Murray, widow	61
Museum of Richmond	5, 42, 52, 53
Nichols, Benedict, Bishop of Bangor	10
Northampton, Helena, Marchioness of	15, 18, 19
Observant Friary, Canterbury	66
Greenwich	65-6
Richmond	65-7, 70
Observatory, Richmond Gardens	23, 49-52, 54
'Old Friars', house at Richmond	66
'Old Palace Place', house at Richmond	66
Osterley, Middlesex	15
Oxford, Carmelite Friary at	65
Palmer, Mr	60
Park(e), Humphry	60
Parliamentary Survey	19, 25, 31, 35-7, 60-4
Pickwelles well	12
Piggot, George	60-1, 63-4
Pole, Reginald, Cardinal	9, 11-2, 15, 36
Prior's Lodging	19, 35, 38, 41, 43, 60
Procurator of Shene	36, 46-7
Queensberry Villas, Richmond	66
Ravensworth, Baron *see* FitzHugh	
Raworth, Robert	71
Recluse monks	7
Reclusory of Shene	8
Red Barn	28, 31, 59
Reeson, John	23, 24
Retreat, The, Richmond	66
Rich, Dr Hugh	66, 73
Richard II, King of England	7, 65
Richmond Gardens	25
Richmond Green	12, 34, 49, 50, 63, 66
Richmond Little Park	17, 19, 59, 63-4
Richmond Lodge	22-24
Richmond Palace	15, 25, 34, 40, 63, 65, 67
Richmond and Lennox, James, Duke of *see* Stewart, James	
Richmond and Twickenham Times	51, 72
Rochester, Sir Robert	9, 12
Rocque, John	25, 41
Rossington, Robert	21, 23
Royal Mid-Surrey Golf Club	50 2
Sackville, Sir Richard	15
Sackville, Thomas, Lord Buckhurst, Earl of Dorset	15, 18
St Albans, Herts	7
St. Helena Terrace, Richmond	66

Scrope, Archbishop 7
Selwyn, Charles 23
Seymour, Anne, Dowager Duchess
 of Somerset 9, 15
Seymour, Edward, Earl of Hertford,
 Duke of Somerset 9, 14, 16, 38, 39
'Sheen Anglorum' 9, 69
Sheen Lane, Richmond 49, 50
Shene Charterhouse
 see Charterhouse of Shene
Shene Palace 7, 65
Shene Reclusory 8
Sidney, Philip, Viscount Lisle,
 Earl of Leicester
 19, 21, 23, 28, 31, 41, 58-9
Sion (Syon) convent 7, 15, 50, 69
'Slawterhous' 41
Somerset, Duke of, Duchess of
 see Seymour
Stables at Shene 19, 36, 39, 62, 64
Stewart, Henry, Earl of Darnley 15
Stewart, James, Duke of Richmond
 and Lennox 19, 64
Stewart, Matthew, Earl of Lennox 15
Stewart, Margaret
 Countess of Lenox 15
Strange, John 10
Suffolk, Duke of *see* Grey, Henry
Surrey Archaeological Collections 5, 52
Sutton, Chiswick, Middlesex 10

Swift, Jonathan 21
Syon House, Isleworth 22, 25, 34, 40
Temple, John 21
Temple, Sir William
 19, 20, 21, 23, 41, 71
Tilman, Anthony 61

Vadstena, Sweden 7
Van Dyck, paintings by 23
Villiers, Sir Edward 19

Walton, Walter 10, 69
Water Gate 39, 62
Water Lane, Richmond 66
Water supply of Charterhouse 12, 62
Watson, Edward 62
Welwey 12
White Cross Tavern and Buildings,
 Richmond 66
William the carpenter
 (of Mount Grace) 10
Wolsey, Thomas, Cardinal 12, 36
Wood, William 61, 63
Worcester, William of
 10, 38, 43, 47, 69-70
Wormall, Mr 28, 59
Wydrington, John, Prior of Shene 10
Wyngaerde, Anthonis van der
 25, 40, 41, 43, 47, 66-7